Leading from the Foundation Up

Leading from the Foundation Up

How Fearing God Builds Stronger Leaders

David M. Cook and Shane W. Parker

Reformation Heritage Books
Grand Rapids, Michigan

Reformation Heritage Books
3070 29th St. SE, Grand Rapids, MI 49512
616–977–0889
orders@heritagebooks.org
www.heritagebooks.org

Printed in the United States of America
23 24 25 26 27 28/10 9 8 7 6 5 4 3 2 1

Library of Congress Cataloging-in-Publication Data

Names: Cook, David M. (Baptist Senior Pastor), author. | Parker, Shane W., author.
Title: Leading from the foundation up : how fearing God builds stronger leaders / David M. Cook and Shane W. Parker.
Description: Grand Rapids, Michigan : Reformation Heritage Books, [2023] | Includes bibliographical references.
Identifiers: LCCN 2022040404 (print) | LCCN 2022040405 (ebook) | ISBN 9781601789815 (hardcover) | ISBN 9781601789822 (epub)
Subjects: LCSH: Leadership—Religious aspects—Christianity. | Fear of God.
Classification: LCC BV4597.53.L43 C66 2023 (print) | LCC BV4597.53.L43 (ebook) | DDC 253—dc23/eng/20221103
LC record available at https://lccn.loc.gov/2022040404
LC ebook record available at https://lccn.loc.gov/2022040405

For additional Reformed literature, request a free book list from Reformation Heritage Books at the above regular or email address.

DEDICATION

For our wives,

Emily and **Lydia,**

Who fear the Lord,
Who are to be praised.

Contents

Acknowledgments

We want to thank God for sending so many people to help us with this project.

The book was strengthened by many friends, colleagues, and church members who reviewed various versions of the manuscript and research it's based on. These include Alex Barrett, Danny Bowen, Michael Ferguson, Leah Hildreth, Morgan Jicka, Raymond Johnson, Jacob Jones, Ross Kearney, Maegan Pittinger, Jonathan Teague, and Paul Webb.

Reformation Heritage Books dedicated time to the manuscript in a season when they and other publishers were overloaded, seeing the book through to the form you're now holding. Joel Beeke helped refine the concepts through conversations and by supplying helpful and hard-to-find source material on the fear of God. David Woollin helped see the manuscript through the review process. Jay Collier helped carry it to print. Annette Gysen gave the manuscript final finishing touches. And Linda den Hollander and Amy Zevenbergen presented it beautifully with typesetting and cover art.

From the depths of our hearts, thank you all. God has been so kind to put each of you in our lives.

Introduction
A Truly Courageous Leader

Armed with this mighty principle,
we shall not play the coward.
—J. C. Ryle

Healthy, courageous leaders are humble, fearful followers. We have written this book to help you see the fear of God as a source of joy and life that fashions people into sound leaders rather than as a strange phrase from another era—or worse, a stern and suffocating way to live. At first mention, these ideas naturally raise some questions. What is the fear of God? What does it have to do with leadership? How would fear make someone courageous or humility make someone great?

These questions are what set us down the path that led to this work. We will answer these and other questions, but before we walk through what we think is the Bible's foundational message about leadership, we want to address a different and darker fear, the one leaders more often lead from—the fear that we won't measure up to other people's expectations.

The Fear of Man

A leadership position, it turns out, is a rather miserable station for someone who needs the approval of others.[1] When we were first called into leadership, neither of us realized how often we would have to disappoint people. I (Dave) had to tell a dear friend that she didn't quite have the voice to sing on our worship team. I'm not sure who enjoyed the conversation less. It wasn't long before I broke the news to a young man that he wasn't ready for ministry. Since I (Shane) began serving in ministry over twenty-five years ago, I've moved from being the wide-eyed, largely clueless, young, pastoral protégé to the ever-learning and humbled-by-failure leader entrusted with the training and care of this generation's emerging Christian leaders. Much has changed in that time, but the fundamental conversations and questions are all too familiar. Aspiring leaders still seem to want mostly affirmation and unchecked congratulation from mentors, so they can become dismayed when I question their motives, actions, and, in some cases, even the authenticity of their calling. After disappointing enough of them, even a leader of leaders who should know better can develop an unhealthy and ironic hunger for affirmation.

This sinful desire for the approval of others often stems from the fear of man. We were made to desire loving relationships, acceptance into a community, and the favor

---

1. Portions of this section first appeared in "Pastors, Fight against Fear of Man by Fighting for the Fear of the Lord," by Dave Cook, Leadership, 9Marks, May 10, 2021, https://www.9marks.org/article/pastors-fight -against-fear-of-man-by-fighting-for-the-fear-of-the-lord/.

of those in authority over us. But the fear of man can multiply and warp these desires into an insatiable hunger for applause, honor, and status.

We can see this dreadful impulse motivate the disciples as they squabble in the upper room. Here, at the unsettling revelation that one of them would betray their master (Luke 22:21–23), they move quickly from interrogating each other to arguing over position. But the argument wasn't over which one of them *was* superior. They fought about which of them would be "*considered* the greatest" (v. 24). Even after seeing the new covenant wine poured and hearing that a traitor lurks among them, they are worried about status!

In this sorrowfully self-absorbed moment, Jesus instructs His disciples. They must see the leader "as the One who serves" precisely because Jesus, their teacher, is "the One who serves," even washing their feet (Luke 22:26–27). By that meek and powerful service, He has provided an inescapable "example" (John 13:12–16) of humble and meek servitude that they are to follow.

If we carry a desire for high regard into leadership, the fear of man creates an unsolvable problem, just as it did for the disciples. It renders us almost completely unable to truly lead. It can make a pastor perform in the pulpit (but not faithfully preach from it). It can make a manager hide in his office with the light off, afraid the bully employee might swing by. It can create an addict-like dependence on fame or internet attention. We can become easily manipulated by those who know how to dole out honor, shame, and pressure.

In the face of these forces and temptations, leadership demands genuine courage. But how do we develop and cultivate such backbone? The answer we hold forth in this book is the fear of God, a glad trembling before God that leads to humility and obedience. Humans were made to revere something. The question isn't whether we will tremble, but at what or before whom we will tremble. This is why we say that a truly courageous leader is a humbly fearful follower. The only leader who won't tremble before the honor and shame of others is a leader who has learned to tremble before God. This leader has found the only fear that will "settle the heart and strengthen the heart against all other fears."[2]

Over the years this trembling disposition will form a person into a courageous and gentle leader. It teaches leaders to sit patiently while a critic scolds them or hurls false accusations at them. Criticism doesn't bother leaders who don't need others to tell them they are successful or great. But that happens only when they are so consumed with God's greatness that they are freed from the enticing fear of man. Yes, fear is actually the key to courage.

I (Dave) have found this especially true in pastoral leadership. No church needs a pastor to meet their expectations or tell them what they want to hear. They need to see a preacher reverently hold up and uphold his Bible. They need to know that I would rather have them all turn

---

2. Jeremiah Burroughs, *Gospel Fear, or, The Heart Trembling at the Word of God Evidences a Blessed Frame of Spirit: Delivered in Several Sermons from Isaiah 66:2 and 2 Kings 22:19*, ed. Don Kistler, 4th ed. (Morgan, Pa.: Soli Deo Gloria, 2001), 35.

against me than utter one word that displeases the Spirit. But to do that with courage and without sin or hypocrisy, I have to learn to fear the Lord daily.

A Tough Sell

We know that grounding courageous leadership in gospel fear probably sounds strange. Aren't the best real-world leaders confident and self-made? Haven't the worst leaders in history used fear to control others? It seems like the last thing a budding leader needs is fear—or God.

Those of us who give this idea a chance may still find another obstacle. The fear of the Lord can be a puzzling concept, even for those who hope in Jesus. Michael Reeves may have summarized this problem best:

> On the one hand, we are told that Christ frees us from fear; on the other, we are told we ought to fear—and fear God, no less. It can leave us wishing that "the fear of God" were not so prominent an idea in Scripture. We have enough fears without adding more, thank you very much. And fearing God just feels so negative, it doesn't seem to square with the God of love we meet in the gospel. Why would any God worth loving want to be feared?[3]

But if we can get past poor examples of leadership and our difficulty in understanding the fear of God, the Bible has a profound and comforting message for all those who know they aren't yet the leader they desire to become. We should

---

3. Michael Reeves, *What Does It Mean to Fear the Lord?* (Wheaton, Ill.: Crossway, 2021), 14.

expect nothing less from a Lord as kind as ours, for all His ways are good.

The Blueprint for Leadership in the Fear of the Lord

Since this book is largely about building leaders, you might find it helpful to think of it as a blueprint, from the foundation up. In the first part, "The Foundation for Leadership," we establish the role of the fear of the Lord as a foundation for good leadership (chapter 1). Then we answer the question you may already be asking: What is the fear of the Lord? (chapter 2).

With these essential pieces in place, we ask why God cares so much about leadership and why He wrote about it so much in the Bible (chapter 3). We solidify the foundation by asking how the fear of the Lord forms the leader (chapter 4). Then we turn to the stories of Saul and David to appreciate the stark contrast between a God-fearing leader and a true coward (chapter 5).

The first part often leaves people wondering how they can learn to fear God. So, between the two parts we've included an interlude that explains how God teaches leaders to fear Him.

In the second section of the work, "Building on the Foundation for Leadership," we look at the ways a foundational fear of the Lord supports pillars of leadership like integrity (chapter 6), wisdom (chapters 7 and 8), and zeal (chapter 9). We also show how the fear of God supports family leadership (chapter 10), justice (chapter 11), and sacrificial service (chapter 12).

God-Fearing Leaders Refuse to Play the Coward

The church and the world need grounded leaders, built brick by brick from the foundation up. Our goal, prayer, and desire are that the Lord might fill the generations to come with steel-spined leaders who humbly and joyfully fear Him.

To live and lead like this, we will all have to keep the future in mind. This Jesus, whom we fear, is coming soon. Commenting on Jesus's words about courage and the fear of the Lord (Luke 12:4–5), J. C. Ryle challenges us to consider how the appropriate fear of our soon-to-return Lord undoes the fleshly fear of man:

> We must supplant the fear of man by a higher and more powerful principle—the fear of God. We must look away from those who can only hurt the body— to Him who has all dominion over the soul. We must turn our eyes from those who can only injure us in the life that now is—to Him who can condemn us to eternal misery in the life to come. Armed with this mighty principle, we shall not play the coward. Seeing Him that is invisible—we shall find the lesser fear melting away before the greater, and the weaker fear before the stronger.[4]

May we, following in Ryle's footsteps, live and lead *now*, in light of *then*, the temporal in view of the eternal.

---

4. J. C. Ryle, *Expository Thoughts on the Gospel of Luke* (New York: Robert Carter, 1875), 60.

PART 1

The Foundation for Leadership

1 The Foundation of Christian Leadership

The trouble with foundations is that we tend to forget about them.

In some ways, that's good. If you're reading this book indoors, you probably aren't thinking about the foundation on which everything around you rests. Even the book in your hands is supported by your arms, which you may have propped on an armrest, which is attached to a chair, which is situated on a floor that rests on the building's foundation. If that foundation were to crack, the whole building might collapse. But you aren't thinking about any of that because you trust the building and its substructure. Someone else did the calculations, drafted the plans, poured the concrete, and knew just how much weight the foundation can bear. They did all of this so that you can sit in a chair and get lost in a book without worry.

You can enjoy a building's shelter without thinking about its foundation. But you can't build a structure without giving focused thought to the foundation. If you did, it wouldn't survive the first windstorm.

Leadership works in a similar way. We appreciate the skills and character qualities our leaders have, often forgetting that those qualities rest on a foundation. If a poorly founded building cannot remain through the earth's shifts and storms, neither can a poorly grounded leader stand through life's twists and turns. So as much as you can enjoy someone else's leadership without thinking much about his or her foundation, you can't become a capable leader or develop another leader without thinking deeply about your own foundation. In this chapter, we will expose the bedrock of leadership so that you can study and master it before you take up the all-important tasks of leading and developing others.

When Christian Leaders Crumble

In the world of architecture, foundational collapse can be abrupt and violent, as construction workers in the suburbs of Shanghai once experienced firsthand. Sprinting through a marathon, they rushed to finish windows and tiled facades of quickly constructed high-rise apartment buildings. Explosive growth in this part of China often pits the need for immediate homes against the need for safe homes. It's easy to see how pressure could lead a builder to use substandard materials or hasty methods.

Cutting corners caught up with the developers right before the tenants moved in. Like a standing domino knocked over by a child's finger, one of the thirteen-story complexes tipped over. It ripped its concrete and rebar foundation from the earth and landed flat on its side.[1]

---

1. While no one was inside the building, one worker was killed. Reuters Staff, "Nearly Completed High-Rise Collapses in Shanghai," Reuters, June 27, 2009, https://www.reuters.com/article/us-china-building/nearly -completed-high-rise-collapses-in-shanghai-idUSTRE55Q0JV20090627.

No one was inside the apartment complex that day (thank God). But when leaders collapse in a similar way, the building is rarely empty. In a sense, people take shelter in leaders and in the ministries they have labored to build only to find that shelter collapsing around them. We often wonder in amazement what happened—"*He was so gifted!*" But without a strong foundation, leaders cannot handle the immense weight of trust.

Interestingly, some building types get by without any foundation at all. In farming communities, landowners often build barns, garages, or woodshops by sinking poles directly into the ground, bypassing the cost of laying a base. While the building may settle oddly and look uneven in twenty years, it's a hay barn, not a high-rise building. The farmers can live with wonky corners if the building holds hay and weathers a summer storm.

Farmers can enjoy the unique charm and live with the architectural frustration of an uneven building if it gets the job done. Many people feel the same way about their leaders. The weight these leaders bear isn't enough to endanger them, but those who take shelter there still observe a few quirks. Whether endearing, overshadowed by other skills, or just plain irritating, the quirks and weaknesses can normally be traced back to a poor foundation.

Many of us have felt the solidity of a strong building. We've jumped up and down but felt no give. We've stood by the window with a cup of coffee to watch a storm roll in. We trust sturdy buildings, sometimes even taking them for granted. People who live with wise, trustworthy leaders can feel much the same way. They sense a resolute sturdiness that enables the whole group to flourish in both sunshine and rain.

Our desire is to help you become that sort of leader by first building a strong foundation and then adding necessary pillars to it. If the load of ten thousand people taking shelter in your leadership rests on you, or the temptations of fame and unaccountability pursue you, or the firing storms of satanic warfare thunder over you, we want you to be left standing and the people who trust you to flourish. But in order to understand the foundation, we first need to look at what God wants from leaders.

What God Expects from Leaders

When people first start leading, they often ask questions like, How do I do this well? or What exactly is my job? For others, these questions arise slowly over years of leading. Googling "how to be a good boss" or "how to lead a team" can get you only so far. There is a nagging sense that a more complete resource—a missing manual—must be out there.

Though the Bible wasn't written to be a leadership manual, it does give us both the foundation and the structure we need to understand and execute leadership. When we survey its requirements for people in authority, a consistent theme emerges. See if you notice it in the discussion of expectations here.

First, God had expectations for Israel's king. In Deuteronomy 17:18–19, Moses makes clear the vision that God has for leadership in His kingdom:

> Also it shall be, when he sits on the throne of his kingdom, that he shall write for himself a copy of

> this law in a book, from the one before the priests, the Levites. And it shall be with him, and he shall read it all the days of his life, that he may learn to fear the LORD his God.

Samuel then echoes these expectations when he anoints Saul, Israel's first king: "If you fear the LORD and serve Him and obey His voice, and do not rebel against the commandment of the LORD, then both you and the king who reigns over you will continue following the LORD your God" (1 Sam. 12:14).

Sadly, Saul didn't measure up. But his successor, David, pleased God and experienced one of the most fruitful reigns in history. On his deathbed he shared the secret to his success: "He who rules over men must be just, ruling in the fear of God" (2 Sam. 23:3). David didn't limit this advice to Israel's kings. Elsewhere, he called rulers all over the earth to the same thing:

> Now therefore, be wise, O kings;
> Be instructed, you judges of the earth.
> Serve the LORD with fear,
> And rejoice with trembling. (Ps. 2:10–11)

God expects the kings of the earth, above all else, *to fear Him*.

This expectation wasn't just for top-level leaders. Jethro advised Moses to appoint "men…such as fear God" to judge Israel under his leadership (Ex. 18:21). Later, Jehoshaphat appointed judges, charging them, "Let the fear of the LORD be upon you" (2 Chron. 19:7), and appointed priests and heads of households with a similar charge to "act in the fear of the LORD" (v. 9). Jesus, stating this negatively, tells a story of an unjust judge who "did not fear God nor regard man" (Luke 18:2).

Nehemiah extended this expectation beyond kings and judges to all the officials in Jerusalem. Angry over oppression in Israel, he rebuked the other nobles and officials: "What you are doing is not good. Should you not walk in the fear of our God because of the reproach of the nations, our enemies?" (Neh. 5:9). He applied the same standard to himself, saying later, "But the former governors who were before me laid burdens on the people, and took from them bread and wine, besides forty shekels of silver. Yes, even their servants bore rule over the people, but I did not do so, because of the fear of God" (v. 15).

God expects a great deal from leaders, but all of it is built on one central piece: *they must fear Him.*

From Expectation to Foundation

We make this claim because as we started researching what people expect from leaders, what God requires of them, and what the Bible has to say about leadership character and competency, we noticed a striking connection. The Bible links the fear of the Lord to everything else it says leaders need.

As students and teachers of leadership, we've had to familiarize ourselves not only with the responsibilities associated with leading others but also with varied leadership models and theories. As we studied these approaches, a major weakness became clear. The Bible's foundation for leadership, the fear of the Lord, is often misplaced or missing entirely.[2]

That's the trouble we have with foundations. We tend to forget about them.

Most leaders today are trained to focus on skills like vision casting, change management, conflict resolution, and team building—all necessary and vital to leadership. But these leaders aren't typically given a reliable compass to direct those skills or formed into the type of person who uses them well. As they develop and perfect these abilities, they can be like homeowners carefully repainting walls and replacing fixtures while their foundation cracks and crumbles beneath them.

It wasn't always this way. Before the twentieth century, leaders were often taught to focus on becoming a virtuous person. Generations before us cherished pillars like integrity in leadership far more than skills. That teaching served them well, to a point. Many God-fearing men and women were able to rise to the call. So were some non-Christians who at least felt they would answer to their god for their conduct and leadership. But the teachings of the day only

---

2. In our research we found two books on leadership that directly address the fear of God: Theodore Roosevelt, *Fear God and Take Your Own Part* (1916; repr., London: Forgotten Books, 2017); and Michael S. Wilder and Timothy Paul Jones, *The God Who Goes before You: Pastoral Leadership as Christ-Centered Followership* (Nashville: B&H Academic, 2018). Both treat the concept meaningfully. It is also common for Christian leadership teaching to emphasize a strong relationship with God as foundational to leadership, though not with the language of the fear of God. We have not found any materials that treat the fear of God as foundational to leadership.

told them the kind of person they needed to become. It did not lay the foundation that helped them to become that person or give them the skills that they needed to succeed.

To paint it very generally, some older models tended to focus on character, and most current models tend to focus on skills. What is missing in both is a foundation.

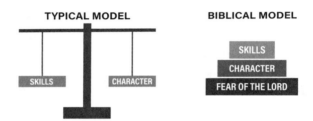

Questions such as "Which is more important: leadership skills or character?" miss the point. Skills should be built on character qualities, and character qualities should be formed in the fear of the Lord. Leadership skills fall like a house of cards when they aren't set on the pillars of wisdom and integrity, and pillars like wisdom and integrity fade without a foundational fear of the Lord.

Much of the blame rests on men like us, teachers of the Bible and of leadership. Those of us who teach leadership have not always made the connection between the foundation, the life, and the skills of the leader. Similarly, in the church we've so neglected teaching on the fear of God (a major theme in the Bible) that many Christians may not even know what it is. As a result, leaders are left trying to learn important skills and develop character qualities with a nagging sense that there must be a vital component that holds it all together.

That crucial element is the fear of the Lord. And so before we draw its connections to leadership, the next chapter answers the question, What is the fear of the Lord?

Discussion Questions

1. What are some activities (e.g., sports, music) you enjoy in which success at a high level is built on sound fundamentals? How is leadership like that activity?

2. Have you been relationally or positionally near when a leader fell into scandal? How big a role do you think foundational failures played in that person's problems?

3. How would you describe a leader's job?

4. Has the leadership teaching you've received so far focused more on skills or on character? What specific advice did it give, if any, on how to grow into a more skillful or moral person?

2 | **The Fear of God**

While the Bible calls fearing God "the whole duty of man" (Eccl. 12:13 ESV), most Christians know very little about it. We hope to remedy that first by clearing up some misconceptions, and then by exploring the Bible to uncover the truth about the fear of the Lord. Though this is a leadership book, the concepts in this chapter can support and enrich all dimensions of life.

What It Is Not: Simply Being Afraid

When you hear the phrase *fear of God*, you may wonder, *Wait, does God want me to be afraid of Him?* The language is confusing because we use the word *fear* differently than we used to. But the English word *fear* can mean anything from warm respect to primal terror. Today we use it mostly when we're afraid of something. But it has often (especially in the past) connoted the respect a son has for a steady father or the admiration an employee has for a great boss. In days long past, we would have said that the young boy bursting with joy while his strong but gentle father lifts him up, holds him tight, and tickles him feels fear for his father. That fear includes awe, security, some glee-filled giggles, and a desire to obey him. This is different, mournfully, from the fear that an abused son would feel for his father.

The words in our Bibles that are often translated *fear* have the same range and flexibility. The same word that speaks of Adam being "afraid" of God's footsteps after eating the forbidden fruit (Gen. 3:10) also speaks of a Messiah whose "delight is in the fear of the LORD" (Isa. 11:3). One fear is frightened and sinful; the other is delighted and faithful. But *fear* characterizes them both.[1] In the New Testament, the women who first learned of Jesus's resurrection ran away "with fear and great joy" (Matt. 28:8). In the whole Bible, fear and joy can be very similar experiences.

So when we think about a phrase like *the fear of the Lord* in the Bible, we have to ask, Which fear? Fortunately, the Bible gives the same clear answer in several places. Fearing God in faith is not the same as being afraid of God, and being afraid of God is not a mark of the Christian life.

When Israel saw the Lord's glory on Mount Sinai—thunder shaking, lightning flashing, the mountain smoking—they were understandably terrified. But Moses said to them, "Do not fear; for God has come to test you... that His fear may be before you, so that you may not sin" (Ex. 20:20). His glory wasn't intended to terrify them; it was supposed to teach them to fear Him. Moses was saying, in essence, "Don't be afraid of God; fear God!"

---

1. For a thorough comparison of many uses of the phrase in the Old Testament, see Bernard Bamberger, "Fear and Love of God in the Old Testament," in *Hebrew Union College Annual* 6 (1929): 39–53, http://www.jstor.org/stable/23502784.

God's presence brings with it a sense of His power, justice, and holiness while also exposing our sinfulness—a good reason to be terrified. But the one who has been forgiven in Christ, brought into His people, and adopted as His child is free to finally love Him. God's power and justice become motivations to rejoice instead of reasons to weep. Any terror before God vanishes, as "there is no fear in love; but perfect love casts out fear, because fear involves torment. But he who fears has not been made perfect in love" (1 John 4:18). Instead of being afraid of Him, we say, "But there is forgiveness with You, that You may be feared" (Ps. 130:4). Terror before God has no place in the heart of a forgiven Christian. This means we have to correct any sense we might have that God wants Christians to be scared or terrified of Him. Only then can we grasp what it means to walk in the fear of the Lord as those who hope in Christ.

What It Is Not: A Dusty Old Testament Idea

The idea of fearing God can also feel, to many, like a relic from another era. The church hasn't taught much about it since the Puritan era, when both the English language and the culture of Christianity were very different. This movement in culture and language can make us feel as if we've moved on from the fear of the Lord, as if it's behind the times.

Some Christians also have an easier time finding the fear of the Lord in the Old Testament—especially in Wisdom Literature like Proverbs and Psalms—than in the pages of the New Testament. That can leave us wondering if Christians have moved beyond the fear of the Lord. Or maybe it's an Old Testament phrase for something the New Testament calls by another name. Admittedly, the idea can seem passé.

But there is a vast difference between outdated and timeless, between last year's paint colors and the *Mona Lisa*. Some things stick around through the ages. The fear of the Lord is both the most ancient of human experiences and the most enduring stance humans will hold. This is because the Lord—who is to be feared—was, is, and is to come (Rev. 1:8).

In fact, the Bible teaches that Christians ought to fear the Lord more completely than ancient Israel did. In one of Israel's darkest hours, prophets rose to promise a new day when God would give His people a new heart, would put His Spirit within them, and would "put My fear in their hearts so that they will not depart from Me" (Jer. 32:39–40; see also Ezek. 11:19; 18:31; 36:26). This new covenant idea was that God's Spirit would transform our hearts so that we would begin to fear Him as we ought. After Jesus ascended to heaven, the Holy Spirit fell on the church, and they began "walking in the fear of the Lord and in the comfort of the Holy Spirit" (Acts 9:31).

This is why in the New Testament God calls Christians to fear Him. As the sage of Ecclesiastes summarized man's duty with "fear God and keep His commandments" (12:13), so Peter says that "whoever fears Him and works righteousness is accepted by Him" (Acts 10:35). In all times God wants the same thing from every person: fear Him and do right. Peter would later write to all Christians everywhere, "And if you call on the Father, who without partiality judges according to each one's work, conduct yourselves throughout the time of your stay here in fear" (1 Peter 1:17); and also, "For this is the will of God.... Honor all people. Love the brotherhood. Fear God. Honor the king" (2:15–17). Knowing God as Father and knowing freedom in Christ should increase our fear. In fact, most of the New Testament's other references to the fear of the Lord come after the Spirit is poured out on the church in Acts 2 (Luke 1:50; 12:5; Acts 9:31; 2 Cor. 5:11; 7:1; Phil. 2:12; Heb. 12:28). We don't fear God *less* because of what Jesus did for us; we fear Him *more*. This gloriously redeemed fear does not drive us away from God; it draws us closer.

This fear will only increase in eternity. When the time comes to reward "those who fear Your name" (Rev. 11:18), an angel will charge every nation on earth to "fear God and give glory to Him" (14:7). We will respond, "Who shall not fear You, O Lord, and glorify Your name? For You alone are holy" (15:4). When the judgment is over, the decree from God's throne will be, "Praise our God, all you His servants and those who fear Him, both small and great!" (19:5). As His glory remains and will only be further revealed, the fear of Him will only become greater and sweeter as the endless ages pass.

What It Is: Awe → Obedience

Here's a brief definition of the fear of the Lord: *trembling deeply before God's glory and walking humbly in His ways.* This definition combines two concepts: awe and obedience.

I (Shane) remember being a kid in the 1980s, holding

my model space shuttle, wearing three-striped athletic socks and Velcro Nikes, visiting Cape Canaveral, Florida. My family and I were just a small part of the huge crowd across the lake from the launchpad. Moms and dads sat in lawn chairs with their children in their laps, all watching wide-eyed. As I held that tiny replica shuttle in my hand, the real, giant NASA craft rocketed upward. The lake rippled. The earth shook at the force blasting against it. Fire and smoke spewed from the bottom of the boosters until the spacecraft began to lift from the ground, hover for a moment, lift faster, and, to the sound of cheers, carry astronauts into the stratosphere. People who have traveled to see launches like this often say they will remember it forever. They leave filled with awe because they have experienced something glorious.

Sadly, the idea of *awe* has fallen on hard times. The word *awesome* is so overused that we might even think less of something called awesome. Something awful is somehow bad (it once meant "full of awe").[2] We might even think that a Christian's heart toward God must be full of something greater than mere awe. But that crowd watching a shuttle lift-off knew what it meant to be filled with awe. True awe makes the body shake and the heart burst with either joy or fright. It makes a soul feel its smallness. There is no greater feeling than joy-filled awe.

---

2. For example, one of Isaac Watts's hymns on Psalm 139 says, "Thy awful glories round me shine, my flesh proclaims thy praise." Isaac Watts, *The Works of the Rev. Isaac Watts* (London: Edward Baines; William Baynes; Thomas Williams and Son; Thomas Hamilton; Josiah Conder, 1813), 9:120.

National parks in the United States give away activity books to children that they can complete while visiting the park and then be sworn in as Junior Rangers—badge and all. At Grand Canyon National Park, one of the activity pages asks the children to look out over the canyon and write down how they feel. The day before his tenth birthday, my (Dave's) son looked over the rim and wrote, "I feel small and happy." Millions of people stand on that rim to stare across that mile-deep canyon because they want the same thing, to feel small and happy.

Awe is what our hearts were made to seek. Films get bigger and better because we want them to leave us in awe. We'll hike all day for one spectacular overlook just to stand for ten minutes in awe of it. We want to see that film, glimpse that valley view, and watch that rocket because they are literally awesome.

Your heart is this way because there is a God in heaven whose glory is worthy of trembling, joyful awe forever—and you were made to worship Him. Your awe-seeking heart was made to be satisfied trembling before Him. This is the first part of what it means to fear God: overflowing with awe as you see some small glimpse of His great glory.

These small glimpses abound when we look for them. You might shake a little as you stand before a deep canyon, the vast ocean, a towering glacier, or the starry sky with your heart full of marvel at the God who created it (Ps. 19:1–6). In those moments, you're fearing God. You might read of the Red Sea crashing on Egypt's army, and you exhale audibly at the safety found in His hand (64:7–10). In your astonishment at God's power, you're fearing

Him. You might imagine Jesus reigning in majesty and tremble with joy (2:11). You might sin (God forbid), taste forgiveness, and then wonder at the God who restores sinners (130:4). You might read His Word, sense its power, and tremble (Ps. 29; Isa. 66:2; Jer. 23:9). You might see the wonder of His powerful works and fear (Hab. 3:2, 16). Your self-absorption will starve as you become wrapped up in the glory of our holy God.

This is the fear of the Lord, the stance of every glad and quivering angel, creature, and soul in heaven, who cries out verses like "Holy, holy, holy is the LORD of hosts; the whole earth is full of His glory!" (Isa. 6:3); and

> You are worthy, O Lord,
> To receive glory and honor and power;
> For You created all things,
> And by Your will they exist and were created.
>   (Rev. 4:11)

If people were to walk daily with this sort of disposition, you might expect they would become humble. Their own greatness would be so overshadowed in their hearts that they could never be wise in their own eyes (Prov. 3:7). This is exactly the sort of change the fear of the Lord brings within a person. A trembling heart is teachable. One who walks in the fear of God becomes humble, quick to listen to His teachings.[3]

Having this teachability leads to the second part of

---

3. Tremper Longman III, *The Fear of the Lord Is Wisdom: A Theological Introduction to Wisdom in Israel* (Grand Rapids: Baker Academic, 2017), 12–13.

the fear of the Lord: joyful obedience. Producing a humility that leads to walking wisely in God's ways, "the fear of the LORD is the beginning of wisdom" (Ps. 111:10). At the same time, obeying God is actually part of fearing Him. He wants you to "fear the LORD your God, to keep all His statutes and His commandments which I command you, you and your son and your grandson" (Deut. 6:2). So obedience both comes from fearing God and is part of fearing God. The Bible speaks of it in both ways.[4]

To fear the Lord, then, is to tremble deeply before His glory and walk humbly in His ways. It is something you will both feel and do as your heart is united to fear His name (Ps. 86:11). It is how you were made to live forever.

The Beginning and the End

We're willing to take it this far: fearing God summarizes everything He wants from you and all humanity. It is both the beginning of wisdom and the end of all things. "Fear God and keep his commandments, for this is the whole duty of man" (Eccl. 12:13 ESV; see also Ps. 111:10; Acts 10:35).

Fearing God is the lifestyle that He designed before we spurned His wisdom and chose to go our own way. To come back to that life, you must first see His glorious holiness, power, and justice—by faith. If you sense His greatness and are aware of your own rebellion against Him, you might put two and two together. You might

---

4. This is why Ecclesiastes 12:13 speaks of fearing God and keeping His commands as a single duty.

realize what a powerful, just, and holy God will do to sinners like us. It may be the most terrifying moment of your life. That's a very different but very real and necessary fear.

But this fear is not what He desires for you forever. He would rather you return (Ezek. 18:23; 33:11; 2 Peter 3:9) and has made it possible. He was willing for His Son Jesus, who delights in the fear of the Lord (Isa. 11:3), to be crushed in your place—the righteous in exchange for the unrighteous (1 Peter 2:24; 3:18; see also Isa. 55:4–5). He stands ready now to forgive your every sin (Ps. 86:5). What you must do is cry out to Jesus for salvation (Rom. 10:13).

We hear a call like this from the soon-to-be rescued thief on the cross. He rebukes his counterpart for mocking Christ, asking, "Do you not even fear God, seeing you are under the same condemnation? And we indeed justly, for we receive the due reward of our deeds; but this Man has done nothing wrong" (Luke 23:40–41). He then pleads that Jesus would remember him when His kingdom is established (v. 42), and Jesus says, "Assuredly, I say to you, today you will be with Me in Paradise" (v. 43).

Those like the condemned thief who desperately place their faith in Jesus will find that God has restored them to joyfully fear Him. As the prophet promises, "I will give you a new heart and put a new spirit within you; I will take the heart of stone out of your flesh and give you a heart of flesh. I will put My Spirit within you and cause you to walk in My statutes, and you will keep My judgments and do them" (Ezek. 36:26–27). You will long to walk in His ways because you will be given

the Spirit of wisdom and understanding,
The Spirit of counsel and might,
The Spirit of knowledge and of the fear of the
LORD. (Isa. 11:2)

That longing may move you to search His Word, praying, "Teach me your way, O LORD, that I may walk in your truth; unite my heart to fear your name" (Ps. 86:11 ESV). You'll see His glory and marvel at it in glad worship. You'll find His teachings and walk in them.

You'll do none of these things perfectly but will grow in the fear of the Lord until He takes you safely to His coming kingdom and finally makes all things new (Rev. 21:5). Then you will hear the final call to worship *and* fear Him (19:5). There you will spend endless ages walking fully in the fear of the Lord, who will reign in visible might, justice, and glory,

for the earth will be filled
With the knowledge of the glory of the LORD,
As the waters cover the sea. (Hab. 2:14)

A Life Well Lived (Is Lived in the Fear of the Lord)

This is the life you were made for, both now and forever: marveling at God's glory and walking in His ways. We're giving our attention here to the fear of God as the foundation of good leadership, but it's really the sure bedrock for all of life. The people who tremble before God so much that their pride becomes consumed by His glory and who live in His ways are the ones who are doing life right. They are the people we want to follow because they are the kind of people we want to be—that is godly leadership.

Discussion Questions

1. Before you read this chapter, how would you have defined the fear of God?

2. Is it ever appropriate to be afraid of God? Explain your answer.

3. Tell about a time when you saw something that filled you with awe. What was it, and what did it feel like?

4. If we carried in our hearts a deep sense of awe at God's glory, how might it change and influence our daily lives?

5. How would you define and explain the fear of the Lord?

3 | Leadership and God's Plan for Human Flourishing

Why is it so important to the Lord that leaders fear Him? Having zoomed in to define the fear of the Lord, now let's pan out to show how it fits into God's great plan for the earth and humanity. God has astonishing plans for us, and God-fearing leadership plays a profoundly key role in them. To get there, we must understand an ancient leadership concept that is less familiar today.

A Ruler's Powerful Image

One of the most striking moments during the Iraq War occurred when the statue of Saddam Hussein fell in Baghdad's Firdos Square in April 2003. It was just a statue, but its removal sent a clear message: Saddam Hussein does not rule here anymore. No longer would the people walking past the city square tremble as they looked up at an image of the dictator's feet and then saw his terrible hand waving above them. The statue was toppled, a symbol of his regime's end.

Rulers, good and evil, often extend and symbolize their rule through images of themselves. They imprint their face on bills and coins throughout the land. Loyal officials hang the royal portrait high and large in their offices. Larger-than-life statues stand over cities. All this reinforces a leader's power and authority. People see the image and remember who is in charge. They may even tremble before the image.

Early readers of Genesis knew this pattern well. They grew up as slaves in ancient Egypt, where pharaohs took this idea even further. The pharaohs claimed that a god ruled Egypt and they were the image of that god. They claimed to extend the rule of the gods and reign as image-bearing representatives, calling themselves covenant sons of the high gods. What blasphemy to claim to be the one living image and son of an invisible god![1]

Now imagine a young Israelite father standing in the dry air of the desert hearing Genesis read for the first time. His family had lived under pharaohs for generations before the living God had ushered them through the Red Sea and sent its waters over Pharaoh and his army. The man holds his young daughter, born into slavery, in his arms as he hears the written words of this living God read aloud: "Let Us make man in Our image, according to Our likeness; let them have dominion over the fish of the sea, over the birds of the air, and over the cattle, over all the earth and over every creeping thing that creeps on the earth" (Gen. 1:26). God had not made one pharaoh to rule *as* His image, but

---

1. The concept of the image of God and its connection to God's plan for humanity are more thoroughly treated in Peter J. Gentry and Stephen J. Wellum, "The Covenant with Creation in Genesis 1–3," in *God's Kingdom through God's Covenants: A Concise Biblical Theology*, by Peter J. Gentry and Stephen J. Wellum (Wheaton, Ill.: Crossway, 2015).

all of humanity to rule *in* His image. His little girl was actually a ruler! Everyone was made in the image of God!

While the father was absorbing this, the next words he would hear were God's commission to "be fruitful and multiply; fill the earth and subdue it; have dominion over the fish of the sea, over the birds of the air, and over every living thing that moves on the earth" (Gen. 1:28). With this charge, God laid out His plan for humanity. Far greater than what the pharaohs falsely claimed to be, all humankind truly is. Humans were created in the image of God to multiply, cover the earth, and rule the earth for Him.

Dominion in God's Image

Most Christians have some inkling of what it means to be made in God's image, a sense that we resemble Him in some ways. We talk about how valuable this must make each human. But we often miss a principal reason we were made in His image: to rule under Him as covenant sons and daughters.

God created all the dazzling stars and galaxies, which our best satellites can barely view. What we long to look into, He holds in His hand. On this one planet, He has given us dominion. Here we turn dirt into buildings, make saltwater drinkable, and till plains into cornfields. We were made in His image so we would accomplish feats of dominion like these.

So to be made in God's image is to resemble Him in some ways. The reason we bear His image is to extend His rule throughout the earth. God made us in His likeness so we could rule the earth for Him.

Reigning as Sons and Daughters

These ideas of image bearing and ruling are connected to another ancient concept: sonship.[2] In the ancient world, your sons ruled under you. At the same time, you might call a servant who ruled under your authority "my son," even though you weren't related.

Parents do something like this today. We often give our children, even at a young age, dominion over a small piece of our home. We might assign them bedrooms, desks, drawers, and eventually cars or even roles in the family business. Parents don't do this to forfeit their authority, but to extend it.

At the same time, we care what our children do with the authority we give them. If we give them their own room, we expect them to keep it clean. If we buy them a dresser, they cannot write "Mom is stupid" on the side of it. The children get some small authority in their parents' house, but they are expected to use it in a way that honors and obeys their parents.

As Christians, we delight that God calls us His sons in the truest and deepest sense. It's also true that, in this limited sense of ruling the earth, every human is a son of God. God the Father has given all humanity small pockets of authority in His creation. And He expects us to rule it in a way that honors and obeys Him.

These two concepts, image bearing and sonship, are closely connected in the Bible. Adam, the first image

---

2. The Bible often uses this term *sons* in the way we do here to refer to both men and women.

bearer, is called "the son of God" in Luke's genealogy (Luke 3:38). He also eventually "begot a son in his own likeness, after his image, and named him Seth" (Gen. 5:3). The Lord tells Pharaoh that Israel, not Pharaoh (the false image of God), is His firstborn son (Ex. 4:22–23). When King David is promised that his sons will rule after him, God says, "I will be his Father, and he shall be My son" (2 Sam. 7:14). Jesus, the Son of God, is called "the image of the invisible God, the firstborn over all creation" (Col. 1:15). Being made in God's image, ruling the earth, and being His son are almost interchangeable ideas.

If God, the sovereign King of all, made us in His image to rule the earth as His sons, we can see why He wants us to fear Him. Sons must honor and obey their father. Princes of the king must heed the king. Those who rule under the Lord must fear the Lord.

Ruling in the Fear of the Lord

That's why the fear of the Lord is called "man's all" (Eccl. 12:13; see also Acts 10:35), and the Bible portrays it as vital to leadership. God wants the ones who rule the trees, waters, animals, farms, rocks, and houses to worship Him and walk in all His ways. He wants the ones who lead other humans to fear Him all the more. Anything else could lead to disaster.

The farmer given dominion over forty acres is called to rule it in the fear of the Lord. If he does, he will cultivate that field according to God's ways and thank Him for the harvest. In the fear of the Lord, he will be diligent to rise early, plow in season, and tend it well. If he has employees, the fear of the Lord will lead him to treat them well and pay them fairly. Tables will be filled because of the work of a God-fearing farmer.

The young couple buying their first home is called to rule it in the fear of the Lord. If they do, they will find the wisdom to maintain it, improve it, and perhaps even raise God-fearing children within it. They celebrate God's sovereignty in their home by ruling it in His image.

Sometimes in God's plan we are even given authority over each other. A college-aged girl given leadership over a children's soccer team is called to coach it in the fear of the Lord. If she reveres and obeys God, she will coach the team according to His ways. God-fearing wisdom will give her the patience to practice and teach the children to practice. She'll speak to the children with clarity, justice, and gentleness just as Jesus would. As she does, she can expect the team to play their best, flourishing under God-fearing leadership. This will generally lead the players to improve and may even help the ball find the net more often.

This is God's design, planted deep in the heart of every person: a court of God-fearing kings and queens who rule the earth as His sons and daughters in His image. The earth should flourish because the children of God rule it well.

Humanity's Poor Track Record

We probably don't have to convince you that humanity's rule over the earth has fallen short of these expectations. Bears, hornets, dandelions, and hosts of other creatures defy us. The earth cries out from our overfishing and chemical dumping while we chase Babel-like dreams of interplanetary life. We worship anything but Jesus and scoff at His ways like a teenager bucks a curfew. This is not the God-fearing rule humanity was commissioned to exercise.

But God's plan, for humankind to rule in the fear of Him, is not thwarted. He will accomplish it through His true Son, who has taken on flesh (John 1:14). He will ultimately and completely accomplish it when Jesus returns, bringing God-fearing rule to the whole earth. In Revelation we see pictures of Jesus ruling on a throne while His people worship Him in joyful fear and reign alongside Him (e.g., 3:21; 7:9–10). The God-fearing Son of God will rule all, while the sons of God will reign with Him.

When Jesus returns to reign, "His delight [will be] in the fear of the LORD" (Isa. 11:3), so He will rule in righteousness. He is not made in the image of God, for He was never made. Instead, He *is* the very image of God (Col. 1:15). The earth will be ruled by a God-fearing human and by God Himself, for Jesus is both human and God.

He will not rule alone, but will be accompanied by His bride, the church: "They shall see His face, and His name shall be on their foreheads.… And they shall reign forever and ever" (Rev. 22:4–5). Humans were made to rule the earth in God's image; the redeemed among us will. We will do so under the true Son and image of God, Jesus the Lord. This is why: "For the earnest expectation of the creation eagerly waits for the revealing of the sons of God" (Rom. 8:19). In its pain, pollution, and carnage, the creation longs to be ruled by God-fearing sons and daughters. Then "the earth shall be full of the knowledge of the LORD as the waters cover the sea" (Isa. 11:9).

We will not rule in our own pride and cleverness, but in the fear of God. He will finish the work He has begun in us, cleansing us of our idols, filling us with His Spirit, and giving us a new heart that is careful to walk in His ways (Ezek. 36:24–27). We will surround His throne in worship, joining with all creation to sing songs like this:

> Blessing and honor and glory and power
> Be to Him who sits on the throne,
> And to the Lamb, forever and ever! (Rev. 5:13)

We will lay our nations' greatest honors down as homage before His feet (Rev. 21:26). We will become the God-fearers we were made to be, unceasingly in awe before His presence and walking in His ways.

Humanity has a profound destiny: to rule the earth in the fear of the Lord. Until then we pray, "Your kingdom come" (Matt. 6:10) and "Even so, come, Lord Jesus!" (Rev. 22:20). Amen.

Hope and Direction for Leaders

This realization gives to any believer and leader who rests in the forgiveness of Jesus two great treasures: genuine hope for tomorrow and trusted guidance for today. Even an elderly believer slowly perishing in a bed, unable to lift a glass of water, can hope to raise a scepter alongside Jesus. That hope can comfort and bolster those who do not expect in this life to rise from their beds again. An abused woman can know that absolute justice will one day "run down like waters" (Amos 5:24 ESV) as she rules in righteous power. She may cry "How long?" now, but one day every tear will be wiped away. Christians who watch their bosses and governments mock God and defy His ways can look forward to a kingdom ruled in reverent justice. Some of today's gardeners will care for vast, unblemished gardens that are unhindered by weeds.

This desire for a better tomorrow is yet another reason to fear our great and merciful God: "Since we are receiving a kingdom which cannot be shaken, let us have grace, by which we may serve God acceptably with reverence and godly fear. For our God is a consuming fire" (Heb. 12:28–29). As God waits to grant this kingdom to us, let us even more live in the fear of Him.

While we wait in that hope, seeing ourselves as the earth's God-fearing rulers also helps us live today. Whether God has given you dominion over one houseplant or four thousand acres of soy, whether one dorm-room dresser or three Fortune 500 companies, He wants you to rule in the fear of the Lord. That means using His wisdom to steward well, walking in obedience to His commands, and living always in worship of Him. When we do, we bring a small glimpse of His coming kingdom to earth today.

One day the kingdom will come and the whole earth will be filled with the fear of the Lord. That's His plan for humanity and the world: a renewed creation ruled by God-fearing sons and daughters. Today, Christians have been given all we need to steward our little kingdoms in the fear of the Lord. In that sense—and in others—the kingdom is already here.

Discussion Questions

1. How would you define and explain what it means to be made in God's image?

2. How might it change your view of yourself and other people to know that God designed humans to be rulers of His kingdom?

3. What has God given you dominion over? How would you describe, in concrete terms, how He wants you to rule it well?

4. When Jesus returns and establishes His kingdom, what might an ideal world ruled by God-fearing kings and queens look like?

4 | How the Fear of God Forms Leaders

Fearing the Lord will strengthen your leadership. But how? How, exactly, would a worshipful posture toward God help you lead more effectively and encourage the people you lead to flourish? This chapter answers that question in two related ways. First, it will form in you the character traits you'll need to lead well. Second, your own fear of God will create an environment in which the people you lead can better reach their God-given potential.

Becoming a Stronger Leader

When you study leadership in the academy, you get to read a lot of good (and some less-than-helpful) leadership books. You also get to sift through the mountains of research on which many of these books are based. As you make your way through that material, you will find some very insightful nuggets of wisdom.

One of these helpful pieces is a series of answers to one of leadership's big questions: What do people want in their leaders? What sort of person would a group freely choose to rally around and gladly follow?

Although substantiated by thousands of hours and millions of dollars in research and writing, it's a surprisingly commonsense answer—people want to follow trustworthy leaders who know what they're doing and believe in what they're doing. We may fall for showstopping leadership, but when people from countries and contexts all over the world sit down and ask what they really want in a leader, they tend to answer the same way: *integrity, wisdom,* and *conviction.*[1]

It is not surprising that leaders self-reflectively ask, "What do people want from me? What would make me a good leader?" We've found that same set of three biblically affirmed traits offers an answer they can remember and a picture that leaders can aim for every day. Your people want you to do what is right, be wise, and believe in something.

Why would the answer be so common? Perhaps it is because the Bible identifies the same key traits for leaders. The Lord calls kings to walk in integrity and church leaders to be blameless. He rewards Solomon's plea to "give to Your servant an understanding heart to judge Your people" (1 Kings 3:9). And He points out the deep convictions of the Bible's most effective leaders. The desire for a leader with integrity, wisdom, and conviction is written on our hearts by the God who demands integrity, wisdom, and conviction from leaders. The world longs for leaders like these because all of creation "eagerly waits for the revealing of the sons of God" (Rom. 8:19). Even if they may not

---

1. We'll present the research underneath this statement in chapters 6, 7, and 9. A more academic treatment of it is found in chapter 3 of "The Fear of the Lord: The Forgotten Foundation of Flourishing Leadership," by David M. Cook (DEdMin thesis, The Southern Baptist Theological Seminary, 2020).

recognize it, the world already longs to be ruled by Christ and His people.

So back to the question we asked at the start of this chapter: How does fearing God make you a better leader? It forms you into a person of integrity, wisdom, and conviction.

Fearing the Lord Changes the Leader

In the Bible, we can trace how the fear of the Lord rests deep within people and changes their outside behavior. It moves them to walk in integrity, gives them wisdom, and develops strong, godly convictions within them. That's important because leadership requires all three.

As we move through the pages of the Bible, we find that the fear of the Lord leads people to depart from evil (Prov. 16:6; see also Job 1:8). In everyday life, we fear the Lord as we "keep all His statutes and His commandments" (Deut. 6:2). A deep sense of God's glory compels us to pay attention to His ways, which leads to walking in them. One biblical word for this is *integrity*.

As we read through the Wisdom Books of the Bible, we find expressions like "The fear of the LORD is the beginning of wisdom" (e.g., Ps. 111:10; Prov. 9:10) scattered among them. As you spend years trembling before God's glory and taking His ways seriously, you should become increasingly *wise*.

Similarly, if we examine the stories of the Bible's most inspiring leaders, we see how they lead from such strong convictions, which have been established through trembling before God's holiness. Joshua's courage, David's love for God's name, Nehemiah's zeal for Jerusalem's wall, Peter's man fishing and sheep feeding, Paul's gospel heralding before the Gentiles—all these stirring examples of conviction were built on their sense of God's great glory. And all those *convictions* inspired the people they led.

We'll unpack each of these ideas in later chapters. For now, we want to develop the big picture. Over years, people who fear God become better people (integrity), become wiser (wisdom), and gain deep values that inform their leadership and inspire others (convictions). In other words, they become better leaders. This is a trembling that somehow makes you stronger, a humility that somehow makes you great.

Let's turn the tables for a moment. What if in five years your boss, your coach, or your pastor had more integrity, was much wiser, and had a stronger God-given sense that the work you do together is important? Would you be more excited about following this leader? Now turn the tables back: the people you lead and serve feel the same way about you.

If you want your leadership to bless people, you will need to be a leader worth following. Many leadership and management books will tell you that in different ways, but we want you to see the source and foundation: the fear of the Lord, by His work and power, will develop those virtues within you.

A God-Fearing Leader Creates a Just Environment

There's another side to this. God-fearing leaders also create the conditions for other people to flourish. Particularly, they create a just environment where oppression and wick-edness don't hinder their fruitfulness.

This is what David taught in his last words:

> He who rules over men must be just,
> Ruling in the fear of God.
> And he shall be like the light of the morning
>   when the sun rises,
> A morning without clouds,
> Like the tender grass springing out of the earth,
> By clear shining after rain. (2 Sam. 23:3–4)

Grass is made to grow upward and outward, but it can do that only in the right conditions. Give it water and let the sun blaze over it, and it will do what it's made to do. You can almost hear the lawn mowers and trimmers of spring and summer whirring.

People are also made to thrive, but we can do it only in the right conditions. Put us in a stable, just environment, and we'll multiply and take dominion over the earth. We'll raise children while we build houses, develop technology, establish farms, and more. But we can do these things to our full potential only when just leaders keep us from cheating one another. This is one reason why humanity's great technological innovations rarely come from countries in turmoil.

According to David, God-fearing leaders are just. But what makes leaders just? Leaders who say in their heart, "God's ways are good," will not just live in them personally but enforce them in the community. They will hold employees who become lazy accountable, pass laws that punish underhanded dealing, and craft and support policies that keep people safe and stop abuse. They will do all that they can to hinder people from wronging one another. Give a leader like that enough power and time to create a just environment, and the whole group will likely benefit.

We can often see this benefit around us. The more a police department can keep drug dealers and gangs off the streets, the freer businesses should be to provide jobs and services. The more a boss can stop abuse and theft in an office, the freer employees are to enthusiastically do their jobs well. The more a coach puts a stop to bullying, the freer players are to work and improve their game. Just leadership should lead to more productivity and happier people.

Changed for Good

Living in the fear of God makes people more righteous, wiser, more deeply convicted of the truth, and more just. It makes them better leaders. The following chapters will unpack each of these ideas more completely. For now, the main question is, What would this look like in real life? It helps to see it rather than simply read about it. For that, the Old Testament offers a vivid picture. The stories of Saul and David were placed alongside each other to give us concrete examples of this very stark difference. So the next chapter examines the opposite pictures of a mighty king who never learns to fear the Lord and a shepherd-turned-ruler who delights in the fear of the Lord.

Discussion Questions

1. If you could choose, what would you want your boss to be like?

2. Talk about a leader you have had who was especially virtuous, wise, or full of zeal and conviction. What was he or she like?

3. If you have ever seen an environment change for the better after a new leader arrived, talk about that. What were the qualities of that new leader? How did the environment change?

5 | A Story of God-Fearing Leadership

The Bible, as beautiful as it is powerful, is made up of many songs, a number of genealogies, a relative handful of letters, some speeches, and a lot of narratives or stories. God loves stories. We love them too. They pull us in, captivate our minds, and teach us wisdom often before we even realize we're being instructed.

This chapter primarily shows how one story, the tale of Saul and David told in the books of 1 and 2 Samuel, brings to life what we've written about so far. While the story of Israel's first two kings sends us through mountains and valleys of joy and heartbreak, it also shows us what occurs when a leader learns to fear the Lord.[1]

The Nerves of New Leadership

We remember the days when we were first called into leadership. What a strange mix of happiness and intimidation. Amid all the joy, there was also a question in the air, one we could see on people's faces but couldn't answer:

---

1. The ideas in this chapter are given academic treatment in David M. Cook, "The King's Fear of the Lord as a Theme in the Books of Samuel," *Themelios* 45, no. 3 (2020): 515–27; and Cook, "Fear of the Lord," chapter 4.

"Will we thrive and prosper with this leader?" It was a new era for the group, but would it be a good and joyful one? The weight was heavy on us as we looked out and saw their faces.

As Saul was crowned Israel's first legitimate king, both he and the people felt the same uncertainty. Saul was so scared that he even ran and hid—so well, in fact, that the people couldn't find him. God had to tell them where he was!

At our pastoral installations, godly men preached to calm our nerves and strengthen our confidence in God. The prophet Samuel did the same for Saul and Israel in their uncertainty. He gave them a reminder, one that is close to the heart of our discussion here:

> If you fear the LORD and serve Him and obey His voice, and do not rebel against the commandment of the LORD, then both you and the king who reigns over you will continue following the LORD your God. However, if you do not obey the voice of the LORD, but rebel against the commandment of the LORD, then the hand of the LORD will be against you, as it was against your fathers. (1 Sam. 12:14–15)

Israel was in for an adventure, but if the people and the king feared God, all would be well.

As prophets did regularly, Samuel was calling Israel to obey the book of Deuteronomy.[2] A good Israelite who heard a prophet declare, "Make sure the king fears the

---

2. Peter John Gentry, *How to Read and Understand the Biblical Prophets* (Wheaton, Ill.: Crossway, 2017), 15.

Lord" would immediately think back to Deuteronomy 17, to God's commands for Israel's king to fear the Lord. A careful look again at Deuteronomy 17:18–20 will give you a checklist of sorts by which you can assess both Saul's and David's reigns:

> Also it shall be, when he sits on the throne of his kingdom, that he shall write for himself a copy of this law in a book, from the one before the priests, the Levites. And it shall be with him, and he shall read it all the days of his life, that he may learn to fear the LORD his God and be careful to observe all the words of this law and these statutes, that his heart may not be lifted above his brethren, that he may not turn aside from the commandment to the right hand or to the left, and that he may prolong his days in his kingdom, he and his children in the midst of Israel.

These expectations for kings follow an "if/then" progression that is familiar in Deuteronomy.[3] *If* the king took a copy of God's Word with him everywhere and read from it daily, *then* he could learn to fear the Lord. *If* he did that, *then* he would keep all of God's laws and treat his fellow Israelites well. And *if* he did that, *then* he would enjoy a long reign and even a long dynasty after him. You might draw it up this way:

---

3. For a helpful treatment of these as well as other elements in Deuteronomy, see Daniel Block, *Deuteronomy*, NIV Application Commentary (Grand Rapids: Zondervan), 2012.

This is all a poetic and detailed way of saying that *if* the king fears God, *then* things will go well.

By calling readers back to Deuteronomy 17 in this way, the text is signaling to us what to watch for in the rest of the story: Will Saul (and later David) learn to fear the Lord? It gives a five-item "God-Fearing King" checklist: (1) How will he treat God's Word? (2) Will he follow all the commands down to the details? (3) Will he keep from mistreating his brothers? (4) Will his reign be long? and (5) Will his sons rule after him? In the remainder of this chapter, we will walk through the story and ask these questions.

The Story of Failing to Fear

Now that we know what to look for, let's walk through Saul's reign. It starts with impressive displays of strength. The Spirit of the Lord rushes on him (1 Sam. 11:6 ESV), and victory with it. We find some hope that Saul might value his countrymen as he spares those who deserve death for slandering him (vv. 12–13). Then come more victories and the accolades of mighty men. His son wins an important battle. Things appear to be going very well.

Then, three years in, Saul faces a test. The Philistine army is gathering, intimidating Israel's army. Some of Saul's men begin to hide in caves; others go AWOL across the fords. Saul feels the pressure to act fast. But he cannot start the battle until he offers sacrifices. And he cannot offer the sacrifices until Samuel arrives, which could take a week.

Saul spends seven sleepless nights waiting for Samuel to come, watching more of his men walk away with every sunrise and sunset. The battle can start whenever Saul commands. All he has to do is break Samuel's instruction and offer the sacrifice himself. Maybe he could begin before too many men leave. But a God-fearing king follows all of God's commands, even when it is difficult. So Saul waits while the ranks of his army diminish.

After seven days, Samuel still hasn't come. It looks like the prophet isn't keeping his end of the deal, not arriving when he had promised. So Saul rose and offered the sacrifice himself. And then Samuel arrived.

Saul tried to explain himself, but there was no excuse. The command may have felt small while the pressure was great, but Saul had violated the Lord's command. So Samuel pronounced a firm word in 1 Samuel 13:13–14: "You have done foolishly. You have not kept the commandment of the LORD your God, which He commanded you. For now the LORD would have established your kingdom over Israel forever. But now your kingdom shall not continue."

Those who have felt the pressures of leadership will also feel for Saul. Why would God care who offers the sacrifice, especially in such extenuating circumstances? The Lord cares because he wants a king who fears Him, and a God-fearing king would take the commands so seriously that even the seemingly small ones would be great in his eyes.

A God-fearing king would be rewarded with a long dynasty, which Saul has forfeited by his action. Now we can cross off three of the items on our "God-Fearing King" checklist.

God-Fearing King Checklist: **SAUL**
- ☐ ~~Treasures God's Word~~
- ☐ ~~Follows All Commands~~
- ☐ Doesn't Mistreat Countrymen
- ☐ Long Reign
- ☐ ~~Long Dynasty~~

First Samuel 12 gave us a standard; by the end of 1 Samuel 13, we can tell that Saul will not meet it.

His failings only get worse in chapter 15. After God patiently urges Saul to "heed the voice of the words of the LORD" (v. 1), He outlines detailed instructions for a battle with the Amalekites. But Saul fumbles the details on this assignment also, leaving many animals and the king alive. Again, Saul failed to take the details of God's commands seriously. God's response is strong: "Because you have rejected the word of the LORD, He also has rejected you from being king" (v. 23). Now we must strike another item off our checklist:

God-Fearing King Checklist: **SAUL**
☐ ~~Treasures God's Word~~
☐ ~~Follows All Commands~~
☐ Doesn't Mistreat Countrymen
☐ ~~Long Reign~~
☐ ~~Long Dynasty~~

In Samuel's responses above, we see again the connections of Deuteronomy 17:18–20. The God-fearing king of Deuteronomy would follow God's commands so that he would have a long reign and a long dynasty. Samuel tells Saul that because he has not followed God's commands, he has lost his kingship and his dynasty.

The Story of a King's Downfall

If looking at Saul's early missteps is like watching a child wreck a bike, reading about his later failings is like watching an engineer derail a passenger train. Once the Lord rejects Saul and the Spirit leaves him, things deteriorate terribly.

Readers can see God's favor move from Saul to David. Tormented by an evil spirit, Saul finds relief only when David plays music. Saul was a head taller than the men of Israel, but little David defeats gigantic Goliath. People begin singing, "Saul has slain his thousands, and David his ten thousands" (1 Sam. 18:7). When Saul saw the fruit of his disobedience, how God's favor had moved to David, the fear of the Lord would have led him to repentance. But Saul's envy led him to try to murder David (vv. 8–11). This evil intent grew into a manhunt that would last the rest of his life, despite David's loyalty to Saul (chapters 18–31).

Saul's rage leads him to abuse not only David but his own son. Suspecting his son Jonathan of treason, he roars over the dinner table, "You son of a perverse, rebellious woman! Do I not know that you have chosen the son of Jesse to your own shame and to the shame of your mother's nakedness?" (1 Sam. 20:30). The next thing he hurled across the table would not be words but a spear, also aimed at his son (v. 33).

Those of us who grew up in safe homes might have a hard time imagining a father saying such a thing to a son, much less hurling a spear at him. But verse 31 makes Saul's motives clear. His dynasty is threatened while David lives. If David is not destroyed, the Lord will have truly taken the kingdom from Saul and his sons, just as He had promised. Saul's abuse of his servant and his son are rooted in his work against the Lord's word, the very word a God-fearing king would cherish.

The same rage directed against Jonathan would later be directed against an entire city of God's priests. For the crime of hosting a faithful servant of the king (David), Saul ordered eighty-five priests executed and the entire city of Nob put to the sword. The order was so egregious that his own servants refused to carry it out. Saul had to command a foreigner to do it.

As we dodge Saul's spear, tremble at his rage-filled words, and view the smoke from the fires of Nob, we can cross the final item off our checklist.

Saul has raged in tyranny over his countrymen, his servants, and even his own son. We are heartbroken but not surprised when Saul's life comes to an end in necromancy and then suicide (chapters 28 and 31).

It's a heartbreak that we should feel deeply because the author is pressing into our hearts and minds the tragedy of a leader who doesn't learn to fear the Lord. Children, parents, leaders, and others are to read his story and wonder what they can do to avoid becoming like Saul. Samuel's connection to Deuteronomy 17 whispers the answer: learn to fear the Lord.

The Story of a Fitting Leader

In the rubble of Saul's tragedy, all eyes turn to David. His conduct so far gives us hope, but we've now been let down by a leader who gave us hope. Will David be different? Will he steward the throne in the fear of the Lord?

His first test comes the moment he learns he has become king. Saul is dead. David could lift up his heart above Saul and Jonathan, boasting of his victory. We might expect a song of triumph, the ringing of tambourines, the beating of drums, and the blaring of trumpets. But this king proves to be different. David's heart breaks for his brothers, the kingdom, and the glory of the Lord.

He lifts up a cry for Israel in 2 Samuel 1:19–20:

> The beauty of Israel is slain on your high places!
> How the mighty have fallen!
> Tell it not in Gath,
> Proclaim it not in the streets of Ashkelon—
> Lest the daughters of the Philistines rejoice,
> Lest the daughters of the uncircumcised triumph.

In verse 23, he lauds both Saul and Jonathan:

> Saul and Jonathan were beloved and pleasant
>   in their lives,
> And in their death they were not divided;
> They were swifter than eagles,
> They were stronger than lions.

And he weeps over the death of the one who sought to kill him in verse 21:

> O mountains of Gilboa,
> Let there be no dew nor rain upon you,
> Nor fields of offerings.
> For the shield of the mighty is cast away there!
> The shield of Saul, not anointed with oil.

And he further laments in verses 24–25:

> O daughters of Israel, weep over Saul,
> Who clothed you in scarlet, with luxury;
> Who put ornaments of gold on your apparel.
>
> How the mighty have fallen in the midst of the battle!

Already we can see a stark contrast between the two kings. At his coronation, Saul's heart feared his brothers, while David's heart loved his brothers, even one who hated him in return. Fearing God, not man, enabled David to love his brothers.

But David's throne would not yet be secured. One of Saul's cousins, Abner, rose to power and brought a great threat to David's future. This threat was removed when Abner was eventually murdered by David's servant Joab. Again, rather than rejoice, David lamented over his fallen brother. He insisted that everyone mourn, and "all the people and all Israel understood that day that it had not been the king's intent to kill Abner the son of Ner" (2 Sam. 3:37). The whole nation could see that he did not lift up his heart above his brothers.

David continued in devotion to his brothers throughout his life. He lifts up one of Saul's house, Mephibosheth (2 Samuel 9). When his own son leads a strong rebellion against him but eventually dies, David mourns for him (2 Samuel 18). Where Saul had hurled abuse toward Jonathan at only the implication of disloyalty, David wails for his truly treacherous son: "Then the king was deeply moved, and went up to the chamber over the gate, and wept. And as he went, he said thus: 'O my son Absalom—my son, my son Absalom—if only I had died in your place! O Absalom my son, my son!'" (2 Sam. 18:33). While Saul's heart pounded with hatred for his brothers, David's heart beat for them.

God-Fearing King Checklist: **DAVID**
☐ Treasures God's Word
☐ Follows All Commands
☑ Doesn't Mistreat Countrymen
☐ Long Reign
☐ Long Dynasty

The Glaring Exception

Yet there is one glaring exception. When Queen Jeze-bel murders Naboth for his vineyard (1 Kings 21), we are appalled. But we aren't exactly shocked. Readers have come to expect that sort of wickedness from Jezebel. But when David commits adultery with a married woman and conspires to murder her husband, we're more than appalled. We're utterly shocked. It's an abuse of power that is disgracefully out of character for David. Can we call it anything other than heinous abuse of his countrymen?

It is here, in David's worst moment, that we see how glaringly different he is from Saul. While Saul shut his ears to the lips of his prophets no matter how gently the cor-rection rolled off them, David's ears hear the storm clouds of the prophet Nathan's thundering rhetoric build into a lightning-strike accusation—and his hard heart breaks.

Nathan tells the story of a rich man with many flocks and herds. Rather than prepare one of his own animals for a guest, he goes to his poor neighbor. He eyes his neigh-bor's lone sheep, beloved like a daughter, eating at the poor man's table. When the rich man steals the poor man's sheep and slaughters it, David is ready to execute him. What a profound way for Nathan to tell the most powerful man on earth, "You are the man!" (2 Sam. 12:7).

Those words are only the beginning of Nathan's stinging rebuke. Yet after a hurricane-force monologue, David's only reply is, "I have sinned against the LORD" (v. 13). He makes no defense of his actions. He accepts dire consequences: rebellion and death in his house. When that rebellion later leads to undeserved scorn, he accepts this also (2 Sam. 16:5–14). There is no entitlement in his repentant heart.

Here we have a profound lesson: God-fearing leaders aren't sinless; they're repentant. They accept the consequences of their sin. They do not act with entitlement when their sin strips from them something they love (including their position). In a moment, they leave their sin behind.

A Long Reign and Eternal Dynasty

We may wonder why David's great sin did not cost him his throne. We would expect that, even after his repentance, someone who had misused his power so egregiously would be disqualified from kingship, no longer worthy of the trust we place in our leaders.

It wasn't that God didn't take David's sin seriously. God's discipline of David was strong. One of David's sons died; another rebelled against him. If his sin was this serious, why didn't he lose the throne? In David's unique case, there is one clear reason: God had promised the throne to him and his sons forever.

When David had resolved to build a temple for the Lord, he was met with a promise. He would not build a house for the Lord, but the Lord would build a house for him!

> Also the LORD tells you that He will make you a house.
>
> "When your days are fulfilled and you rest with your fathers, I will set up your seed after you, who will come from your body, and I will establish his kingdom. He shall build a house for My name, and

I will establish the throne of his kingdom forever. I will be his Father, and he shall be My son. If he commits iniquity, I will chasten him with the rod of men and with the blows of the sons of men. But My mercy shall not depart from him, as I took it from Saul, whom I removed from before you. And your house and your kingdom shall be established forever before you. Your throne shall be established forever." (2 Sam. 7:11–16)

For David and his sons, grievous sin would mean strong discipline but not the loss of the kingdom. This explains why God took David's sin seriously but did not take the throne from him. It also helps us compare David to the ideal of Deuteronomy 17. His sons would rule forever. His greater son, Jesus, still reigns today.

God-Fearing King Checklist: **DAVID**
- ☐ Treasures God's Word
- ☐ Follows All Commands
- ☑ Doesn't Mistreat Countrymen
- ☑ Long Reign
- ☑ Long Dynasty

David is shaping up to be the king that Deuteronomy described.

Walk in the Lord's Ways

Toward the end of his life, David began to speak more openly of his leadership. We often ask veteran, successful leaders what their secret was. David gave his answers:

The LORD rewarded me according to my
  righteousness;
According to the cleanness of my hands
He has recompensed me.
For I have kept the ways of the LORD,
And have not wickedly departed from my God.
For all His judgments were before me;
And as for His statutes, I did not depart from them.
I was also blameless before Him,
And I kept myself from my iniquity.
Therefore the LORD has recompensed me according
  to my righteousness,
According to my cleanness in His eyes.
  (2 Sam. 22:21–25)

Saul lost his kingship and his dynasty because he did not keep the words of the Lord. David maintained them because he "kept the ways of the LORD."

God-Fearing King Checklist: **DAVID**
☑ Treasures God's Word
☑ Follows All Commands
☑ Doesn't Mistreat Countrymen
☑ Long Reign
☑ Long Dynasty

There was a reason David walked in the Lord's ways— because he valued the Lord's word:

> As for God, His way is perfect;
> The word of the LORD is proven;
> He is a shield to all who trust in Him. (v. 31)

By this point, most readers are right where the writer

wants them. David is the king, even the man, Saul was not. There must be a foundation to all this, to David's love for the Lord's word and steadfastness in the Lord's ways.

Indeed, there is. As David's life draws to a close and the deathbed sheet is pulled up over him, he reminds us of what made the difference. His leadership shone "like the light of the morning when the sun rises," sprouting Israel "like the tender grass springing out of the earth" because he ruled "in the fear of God" (2 Sam. 23:4, 3, respectively). With these words, we see that David fulfills every dimension of Deuteronomy 17:18–20.

Deuteronomy taught us to expect it. As David dies, he reminds us of the one quality that holds together a leader's integrity, love for others, and blessing to others: the fear of God. David isn't just the good king Saul was not. He is the God-fearing leader Saul was not. Until his greater son, Messiah, would come, David lived in Israel's memory as the model of a God-fearing leader and the flourishing that comes with it.

While principles ground our thinking and ideals, biblical stories bring these principles to life and move us to action. This story makes us feel the weight of the concepts we discussed earlier and see how they might play out in our own lives and leadership.

In my (Dave's) life, this is a story that showed me how much I need to grow in the fear of the Lord every day. Our fourth baby would cry through the night, challenging my favorite habit of getting up an hour before the children to read my Bible and pray. Sacrificing even more sleep to read with blurry eyes and offer tired, incoherent prayers would do me no good, I reasoned. But I could feel Saul's sword poking me before the sun rose, reminding me of what I may become tomorrow if I neglected God's Word today.

Our prayer is that the story of Saul and David does something similar for you. We want every leader to see that the source of our growth as leaders, as men and women of God, and in the fear of the Lord lies in a Book some of us leave closed on our bedside tables. The Lord's directive to the king was that "he shall read it all the days of his life, that he may learn to fear the LORD his God and be careful to observe all the words of this law and these statutes" (Deut. 17:19). May those words be ever true of you.

Discussion Questions

1. Which of Saul's tendencies reminded you of leaders you have served with? Which ones reminded you of yourself?

2. Which of David's good tendencies reminded you of leaders you've known?

3. Which other kings of Israel or Judah fulfilled, positively or negatively, the instructions to kings in Deuteronomy 17:14–20? Explain your answer.

4. Which of the concepts in the previous chapters became clearer after seeing them in the stories of David and Saul?

Interlude
How God Teaches Us to Fear Him

Before we move into the nuts and bolts of how the fear of the Lord affects leadership, we want to consider what you can do to grow in it. We've mentioned pieces of this throughout the book, but here they are together.

How God Teaches It

This may sound obvious, but it's easy to miss: the fear of the Lord starts with the Lord. We cannot marvel before His glory if He does not show us that glory. And even where He does reveal His glory, what we do with it can often be tragic. Here's a look at what humans are prone to do when God shows them His arresting glory: "Although they knew God, they did not glorify Him as God, nor were thankful, but became futile in their thoughts, and their foolish hearts were darkened. Professing to be wise, they became fools, and changed the glory of the incorruptible God into an image made like corruptible man—and birds and four-footed animals and creeping things" (Rom. 1:21–23). We see God's glory every day but naturally recoil against it and reject it. We would rather worship something else. As long as our hearts remain so hardened against Him and His beauty, we won't learn to fear Him.

God begins teaching us to fear Him again by giving us a new, soft heart and the Spirit of the fear of the Lord (Ezek. 36:26; see also Isa. 11:2). This is what awakens us and, through the good news of Jesus, brings us into new life in the fear of the Lord.

Without the Holy Spirit and new life in Christ, it's still possible to sense God's worthiness to be worshiped and obeyed, and it's even possible to live like all that we do will one day be judged. Many people live this way, and sometimes they are called God-fearing. Like the scribe who asked Jesus what the greatest commandment was, they are often not far from the kingdom of God (Luke 12:28–34).

But to enter and be restored to the God-fearing life, we must be born again (John 3). We must be given a new heart that trusts Jesus for forgiveness, longs to worship before His glory, and desires to walk in His ways.

All this is to say that if you are a Christian, God has started the work by revealing His glory to you and giving you a new heart that longs to fear Him. You have work to do, but God has given you what you need to do it.

How We Learn It

As a teacher, God does His part and shows you your part. Your part is simple to learn but slow to master—like learning to play a sport. You learn to fear Him by responding to His word rightly: seeking His glory to marvel before it and seeking His ways to walk in them. Instructions for how to achieve both are most readily available in his written word, the Bible.

This is why the king is told to read his copy of God's law every day so "that he may learn to fear the LORD his

God" (Deut. 17:19). If you want to see God's glory and learn His ways, they are both there on every page. This is also why the most blessed person is the one who reads and thinks on God's written words "day and night" (Ps. 1:2).

The best way to grow in the fear of the Lord is to read from the Bible every day, looking for God's glory and God's ways. Because the gospel is the most profound display of God's glory and because by it alone can we be restored to His ways, you should also look for the gospel. Where you see God's glory—anything that makes you think *Wow!* about God—stop and worship Him. Where you see His ways, turn from sin and walk in them. Where you see the gospel, embrace it. A renewed heart that does this every day will turn from evil (Prov. 3:7) and walk in spiritual life (Ps. 1:3).

There are many ways daily Bible reading can be done. Reading four chapters each day will take you through the whole Bible in less than a year, and there are many daily Bible-reading plans to help. Or you could focus on one chapter each day and spend three to four years walking more slowly through the Bible. You could pick one book of the Bible and spend months reading it ten times, sometimes one paragraph a day and sometimes several chapters a day. You can try to memorize chapters or entire books (children are great at this). Because the Wisdom Books are good to sprinkle on every reading like salt on every dish, you can spend thirty seconds memorizing one proverb every day after your reading is done. Many people read five psalms and one chapter of Proverbs before bed each night, which takes them through both books every month.

The options are nearly endless, but the important thing is to set a daily time, find a place, and stick to it. If you read the Bible every day, marveling when you see God's glory, obeying when you see His ways, and embracing the gospel, you'll grow in the fear of the Lord.

Discussion Questions

1. In Romans 1, Paul emphasizes that when humans see God's glory, they naturally reject it and refuse to worship Him. When have there been times you've seen God's glory in creation but not worshiped Him?

2. Do you read the Bible daily? If so, when and how do you do it?

3. Which of the ideas in this interlude would enrich your Bible reading?

4. What is your plan for growing in the fear of God through daily Bible reading and worship this month, quarter, or year?

PART 2

Building on the Foundation for Leadership

6 | Earning Trust through God-Fearing Integrity

When people say they want good leadership, what do they really mean? We introduced our answer in part 1: people want to follow trustworthy leaders who know what they're doing and believe in what they're doing. The next four chapters unpack that idea. We'll look at integrity (trustworthy leaders), wisdom (who know what they're doing), and convictions (and believe in what they're doing). We'll see how necessary all three are to leadership and how the Bible grounds them in the fear of the Lord. Then we'll look at other pillars of leadership in the same way.

This chapter is about the first part of that sentence, being a trustworthy person. The more authority and influence you have, the more others are counting on you to do the right thing. Since higher-level positions tend to come with less accountability and more power, we count on our leaders not to betray us or act corruptly when no one is looking. The character quality we're looking for is called *integrity*: a catchall word for a well-rounded character.

Defining Integrity

Anything complicated—a car, a house, or a computer—needs to have integrity to work properly. If many parts all depend on each other, then every piece needs to function for the whole thing to function. If your computer's screen stops working, the keyboard won't be all that useful either. But if everything works, the whole machine has integrity and is useful.

A person's moral integrity works the same way; every piece of a person's character depends on the others. A mostly trustworthy person who regularly erupts in anger doesn't have integrity. Neither does a mostly ethical man who cannot control his sexual appetite. To have integrity, one must have complete character with no major defects.

The Old Testament words used for integrity refer to completeness of character and purity of heart.[1] They don't necessarily mean "sinless," but that the person's character is without major flaws and motives aren't mixed. It's used of David, who shepherded Israel "according to the integrity of his heart" (Ps. 78:72), and of Job, who held on to his "integrity" (Job 2:3, 9). In the New Testament, the same concept is used of the sound teaching Titus was to give Cretan churches (Titus 2:7). None of these men were sinless, but they led with pure intentions and showed complete, well-rounded character.

---

1. Ludwig Koehler and Walter Baumgartner, "תֹּם," in *The Hebrew and Aramaic Lexicon of the Old Testament*, trans. and ed. M. E. J. Richardson (Leiden, Netherlands: Brill, 2000), Logos Bible Software; Koehler and Baumgartner, "תֻּמָּה," in *Hebrew and Aramaic Lexicon of the Old Testament*; and Fredrick William Danker and Walter Bauer, s.v. "Ἀφθορία," in *A Greek-English Lexicon of the New Testament and Other Early Christian Literature* (Chicago: University of Chicago Press, 2000), Logos Bible Software.

God Requires Integrity from Leaders

This consistent, well-rounded character is essential for leadership. Crowds should not gather in the shelter of an incomplete or unmaintained building. They wouldn't be safe there. Neither should a group be entrusted to a leader with incomplete character, whether that person is prone to lying, drunkenness, sexual sin, or some other vice. If you want people to trust you, you have to show them you are trustworthy by leading them honestly.

This is why God requires integrity from leaders. The main measure of Israel's kings is whether they walked "as [their] father David walked, in integrity of heart and in uprightness" (1 Kings 9:4).[2] Moses was counseled to appoint judges who were "men of truth" (Ex. 18:21).[3] Titus and Timothy were instructed to appoint elders who were "blameless" and deacons who were "reverent" (1 Tim. 3:2, 8; Titus 1:6).[4]

The World Is Starved for Leaders with Integrity

If the desire for integrity in leadership sounds like common sense, plenty of research shows just how common that sense is. We may fall for showstoppers or get sucked into cults of personality, but when we truly reflect on what we want our leaders to be like, we almost always want them to be virtuous people.

---

2. Compare with 1 Kings 15:26, 34; 16:2, 19; 22:52; 2 Kings 8:18, 27; 16:3; 21:22; 2 Chron. 20:32; 28:2; 34:2.

3. These judges also needed to "fear God."

4. Both passages go on to describe complete, well-rounded character. The Titus passage does not include deacons.

Some researchers have surveyed the US population and even assessed global samples[5] to ask what qualities people want in leaders and study how those expectations change from place to place. People's expectations of their leaders vary in different parts of the world, enough to make cross-cultural leadership challenging. But what's even more striking is how much is the same from place to place.[6]

Some books have taken the qualities that every culture looks for in a leader and simplified them into a clear picture of a person who could, presumably, lead anywhere.[7] We boil it down to that now-familiar sentence: people want to follow trustworthy leaders who know what they're doing and believe in what they're doing.

In each of these leadership studies, a quality like integrity or honesty consistently sits at the top of the list. Strong character "makes a leader believable and worthy of

---

5. Barry Z. Posner and Warren H. Schmidt, "Values and the American Manager: An Update," *California Management Review* 26, no. 3 (1984): 202–16; Posner and Schmidt, "Values and Expectations of Federal Service Executives," *Public Administration Review* 46, no. 5 (1986): 447–54; and Suzanne Bates, *Speak Like a CEO: Secrets for Commanding Attention and Getting Results* (New York: McGraw Hill, 2005), 203–9.

6. Peter W. Dorfman, Paul J. Hanges, and Felix C. Brodbeck, "Leadership and Cultural Variation: The Identification of Culturally Endorsed Leadership Profiles," in *Culture, Leadership, and Organizations: The GLOBE Study of 62 Societies,* ed. Robert J. House et al. (Thousand Oaks, Calif.: Sage, 2004), 669–719; and Steelcase, *Worldwide Office Environment Index Summary Report* (Grand Rapids: Steelcase, 1991).

7. M. Kouzes and Barry Z. Posner, *The Truth about Leadership: The No-Fads, Heart-of-the-Matter Facts You Need to Know* (San Francisco: Jossey-Bass, 2010); and Peter G. Northouse, *Leadership: Theory and Practice*, 7th ed. (Los Angeles: SAGE, 2015). Northouse summarizes the GLOBE study accessibly in this volume.

our trust."[8] If you act with double motives, don't do what you say you will do, and ignore your character flaws, why should people trust you?

This trust is the very currency that leaders deal in every day. Seasoned leaders often speak of trust like a bank account. Earn the trust of the people you lead, and you're making a deposit into the account. Require something difficult of them (which you will necessarily do), and you're making a withdrawal. The idea is to always have plenty of funds in the account.

The Close Connection between Integrity and the Fear of the Lord

Steven Covey once famously surveyed hundreds of leadership books and "success literature" throughout US history and uncovered an interesting trend. For the first 150 years of US history, the books tended to laud integrity as the core of sound leadership. But in the twentieth century, the emphasis shifted from this "Character Ethic" to a "Personality Ethic."[9] Today we see both types of books—some that focus on a leader's character and others that focus on personality and skills. The difference is strong enough that one can almost divide leadership writings into two subgenres. Covey's work showed that integrity is something of a lost value in American culture today. But people resonated

8. Northouse, *Leadership: Theory and Practice*, 25.

9. Stephen R. Covey, *The Seven Habits of Highly Effective People: Restoring the Character Ethic*, 25th anniversary ed. (New York: Simon & Schuster, 2013), 26–27.

with his message, which showed how timeless the call for integrity in leadership is.

Some people would look at this trend and call for a return to the old days of character-driven leadership. But we call leaders further back (and forward) to humanity's original design. Yes, leadership depends on integrity. But integrity is built on the fear of the Lord. The church cannot expect to raise up leaders with integrity until it recovers robust teaching on the fear of God.

The Bible makes this connection between integrity and the fear of the Lord in several texts. These passages give the sense that the fear of the Lord develops integrity within a person but also that the two are one. The connection is mysterious, but we can at least say that if you want to grow in integrity, you must learn to fear the Lord.

The author of Job introduces him in this way: "That man was blameless and upright, and one who feared God and shunned evil" (Job 1:1). The Lord Himself also describes him twice as "a blameless and upright man, one who fears God and shuns evil" (Job 1:8; 2:3). Job's friend later asks him in parallel speech, "Is not your reverence your confidence? And the integrity of your ways your hope?" (Job 4:6). Job's integrity and his fear of the Lord are spoken of as if they were the same thing.

The law also connects the two ideas. It sets fearing God and wronging others as opposites when it says, "Therefore you shall not oppress one another, but you shall fear your God; for I am the LORD your God" (Lev. 25:17). Elsewhere, the law calls Israel to "fear the LORD your God" and tells them how: "Keep all His statutes and His commandments which I command you" (Deut. 6:2). Often the Bible places different words for the two ideas together, saying, "You shall walk after the LORD your God and fear Him, and keep His commandments and obey His voice; you shall serve Him and hold fast to Him" (13:4). One can see in these verses the close connection between the two and at times the way that fearing God leads to walking in integrity.

Additionally, the book of Proverbs teaches us something of how the fear of the Lord helps us walk rightly. The writer pulls back the curtain slightly on the mysterious connection. Early on, the sage writes, "Do not be wise in your own eyes; fear the LORD and depart from evil" (Prov. 3:7). Here and in the surrounding verses, fearing God is seen as the opposite of being prideful. The arrogant see themselves as wise, so they look on God's teachings with boredom. We wouldn't expect them to learn God's ways as they roll their eyes through sermons and scoff through Bible readings. But the one who trembles before God's word becomes humble enough to listen. In the fear of God, they study His ways and learn them. Then they walk with an acute awareness of this glorious God whose eyes are always on them. In that way, "by the fear of the LORD one departs from evil" (Prov. 16:6).

Integrity and the fear of the Lord, then, have a deep and mysterious connection. In a sense, fearing God and walking in integrity are the same thing. In another sense, fearing God results in integrity. From yet another angle, walking in integrity is how we fear the Lord in everyday life. From every angle, leaders who want to grow in integrity must learn to fear the Lord.

The Inevitable Danger of Unaccountability

We believe the current integrity crisis in Western leadership is rooted in the absence of the fear of the Lord. People who do not tremble before God are not likely to do the right thing in a pivotal moment when everyone's back is turned. In that moment, they do not sense that God is watching.

If the church proclaims a small version of our glorious God, fails to call for repentance, teaches leaders to focus on skills, gathers around the ones who have the best knack for drawing a crowd, and keeps them at an unaccountable, celebrity-like distance from the people they lead, it should expect Satan to have an easy time scandalizing those leaders. Inasmuch as we have neglected to teach leaders to fear God, we have primed them for scandal and fall at the claws of our prowling, roaring enemy (see 1 Peter 5:8). Inasmuch as the church follows Western culture into secular assumptions and senses no God worth fearing, it will produce leaders long on craftiness and short on integrity. William Gurnall's warning will ring ever true: "Unholiness in a preacher's life will either stop his mouth from reproving, or the people's ears from receiving."[10]

What is the solution? The church must show the world a better way by raising up young leaders who sense the eyes of Jesus on them when they are all alone. What is missing in both the church and the world is the fear of God. We need so desperately men and women who tremble before

---

10. William Gurnall, *The Christian in Complete Armour* (Glasgow: Blackie and Son, 1865), 2:579.

a God who will always hold them to judgment, who truly believe that God's ways are good. Only these leaders will understand that they are always accountable. Only they are worthy to lead our churches, governments, businesses, and homes.

When leaders do fall, their inner circle must fear God by holding them accountable. This is a courageous and often costly step that may end painfully for the one who does right. But who else would take it besides the one who fears God more than the powerful?

Leadership will always be a position of trust, and so it requires trustworthy people. But trustworthy people are not born; they are formed. As their hands and feet tremble, they begin to stand strong in integrity.

This means that if you want to become trustworthy tomorrow, you must learn the fear of the Lord today. Your disposition when you read your Bible today affects how you will handle fateful moments of unaccountable temptation tomorrow. If you want to get your walk right, you must get the posture of your heart right. Tremble before God's word, learn His ways, and walk in them. Then you will know integrity, which would bless all those you lead.

Discussion Questions

1. How would you define *integrity*?

2. What are some areas you need to grow in or sins you need to repent of before you can say that you have a well-rounded character? Think of someone in your life you could ask for an honest answer to this question.

3. Tell about a leader you've worked with who had an especially strong character or who had major gaps in his or her character. How did that make it easier or more difficult to trust that person? How did that affect your relationship?

4. How would you describe the connection between the fear of the Lord and integrity?

7 | Leadership Skills Built on God-Fearing Wisdom

People want to follow trustworthy leaders who know what they're doing and believe in what they're doing. This chapter is about the second element of that statement; it is about *wisdom*.

If you've ever been responsible for leading other human beings, you've probably felt out of your depth. How do you manage so many varied personalities with all their quirks and expectations? How do you handle conflict when you can't tell who's telling the truth? How do you lead a group to strategize and innovate in an area that you may not fully understand yourself? How do you make the right call when hard times come and people look to you for the courage to make complex and difficult decisions? Leaders are constantly faced with the hard truth that we aren't wise enough for this gig.

Leadership Requires Wisdom

Solomon felt the heaviness of this burden when he ascended Israel's throne. That's when God made him the ultimate better-than-a-genie-in-a-bottle offer: "Ask! What shall I give you?" (1 Kings 3:5). What would you ask for if

God offered to grant you anything? Plenty of overwhelmed leaders would say just what Solomon said:

> Now, O LORD my God, You have made Your servant king instead of my father David, but I am a little child; I do not know how to go out or come in. And Your servant is in the midst of Your people whom You have chosen, a great people, too numerous to be numbered or counted. Therefore give to Your servant an understanding heart to judge Your people, that I may discern between good and evil. For who is able to judge this great people of Yours? (vv. 7–9)

Solomon knew precisely what to ask for. God was so pleased with Solomon that He gave not only wisdom but also riches and honor. Solomon became the world's greatest sage, with kings and queens sitting at his feet. He also became Israel's most prosperous king, earning in excess of fifty thousand pounds of gold each year (1 Kings 10:14–15). But Solomon treasured his wisdom over mountains of gold. He later wrote to his sons,

> Happy is the man who finds wisdom,
> And the man who gains understanding;
> For her proceeds are better than the profits of silver,
> And her gain than fine gold.
> She is more precious than rubies,
> And all the things you may desire cannot compare
>   with her. (Prov. 3:13–15)

Solomon understood what all leaders must understand: leadership requires wisdom. Wisdom says,

> By me princes rule, and nobles,
> All the judges of the earth.

I love those who love me,
And those who seek me diligently will find me.
(Prov. 8:16–17)

We think of Proverbs as a wisdom manual—and it is, in part—but Solomon wrote and collected these proverbs as a leadership guide, a king writing to the sons who would rule after him.[1]

How do leaders build teams and keep them together? How do they lead productive conversations and arrive at solid decisions? How do they evaluate candidates during interviews and hire the right people? Wisdom says, "By me princes rule." They do it through godly wisdom.

Giving the People What They Want (and Need)

The broader world seems also to understand that leadership requires wisdom, though they may not always use the word. Of the surveys we've mentioned before, the GLOBE study found that people of cultures spanning the globe desire leaders with many qualities the Bible commends as wise. All cultures want leaders who are dependable, intelligent, informed, skilled in administration, able to plan ahead, communicative, good coordinators, team builders, excellence oriented, win-win problem solvers, good bargainers, and decisive.[2]

---

1. I (Dave) am indebted to Jon Akin, my former pastor, whose preaching helped me see Proverbs this way. Jonathan Akin, *Exalting Jesus in Proverbs*, Christ-Centered Exposition (Nashville: Holman Reference, 2017).

2. Dorfman, Hanges, and Brodbeck, "Leadership and Cultural Variation," 677.

American professionals generally indicate that they want leaders who have knowledge, can listen and communicate, and will follow through.[3] They want leaders with competence and a forward-looking orientation.[4] You can sum up all these qualities and more with one biblical word: wisdom. Perhaps that is why the *Oxford Handbook of Leadership* says wisdom may be the most important and rarest quality in leadership.[5]

There is so much involved in learning wisdom, but the Christian leader has more than enough help. You may not have enough wisdom in yourself to lead well, but you have access to a God who has it all and loves to give it away.

The Wisdom of Living Well

If we had to simply define *wisdom*, it boils down to "being good at life." It's living a moral life, knowing how the world works, and being adept at the skills of life. This intersects with two parts of our axiom: people want to follow trustworthy leaders who know what they're doing and believe in what they're doing. Wisdom helps you become a trustworthy person who knows what you're doing.

This is why the Proverbs teach us about "the instruction of wisdom" and also about "justice, judgment, and equity" (1:3). On one page they give us morals like, "Treasures

---

3. Bates, *Speak Like a CEO*, 207–9.

4. James M. Kouzes and Barry Z. Posner, *Credibility: How Leaders Gain and Lose It, Why People Demand It*, Jossey-Bass Management Series (San Francisco: Jossey-Bass, 1993), 13–18.

5. Michael G. Rumsey, ed., *The Oxford Handbook of Leadership*, Oxford Library of Psychology (New York: Oxford University Press, 2013), 55.

of wickedness profit nothing, but righteousness delivers from death" (10:2). On the next page we read, "There is one who makes himself rich, yet has nothing; and one who makes himself poor, yet has great riches" (13:7). And on the next page, we find pro tips like, "Without counsel, plans go awry, but in the multitude of counselors they are established" (15:22). Add up the morals, the insight, and the sage advice, and you have a person who knows how to live life well—a wise person.

The Source of Wisdom

But before the Proverbs get into the details of wisdom, they tell us where to seek it. After spending a chapter making us long for wisdom, the sage says that if we long for it we must understand the fear of the Lord:

> For the LORD gives wisdom;
> From His mouth come knowledge and
>   understanding;
> He stores up sound wisdom for the upright;
> He is a shield to those who walk uprightly;
> He guards the paths of justice,
> And preserves the way of His saints. (2:6–8)

To those who fear the Lord and seek understanding from Him, He gives a wisdom that guards them in life's most trying situations. If you want wisdom, go to the ever-wise source, the Lord Himself.

Not only is He full of wisdom but He loves to give it to those who seek it. James says so refreshingly, "If any of you lacks wisdom, let him ask of God, who gives to all liberally and without reproach, and it will be given to him"

(James 1:5). This is the generous God Solomon experienced when he asked for wisdom. God, delighted that Solomon asked for wisdom, gave it to him abundantly. The Lord's heart isn't a trickle of life-giving wisdom; it's a streaming hydrant.

He loves to give wisdom so much that He wrote an entire book about it. But, of course, the Proverbs can't contain all His wisdom. It must spill out into other Wisdom Books like the Psalms, Song of Solomon, Job, and Ecclesiastes, and then to the whole Bible. Even then, we know only a portion. To seek wisdom in God's Word is like trying to catch the rain: you won't catch all the drops, but you'll get drenched. The source of this downpour is the Lord Himself.

The Heart of Wisdom

So wisdom comes from God, but it doesn't go to everyone, everywhere. It goes to a particular place: into a heart that fears Him. As the Wisdom Books repeat their refrain, "The fear of the LORD is the beginning of wisdom" (Ps. 111:10).

We can see from our earlier discussions how this works. A heart overtaken by God's glory would be, we expect, no longer wise in its own eyes (Prov. 3:7). It would become teachable, marveling at God's wisdom. It would see the way God wisely set up creation, crafted the depths, shaped the mountains, fashioned the fields, scattered the stars, spun the clouds, carved the coastlines, and fixed the ground (Prov. 8:22–31). Amazed, the God-fearer would seek God's wisdom and walk in it.

As God loves to write down His wisdom and grant it

to people, the God-fearer will read it regularly and ask for it constantly. This is how God-fearing leaders grow in wisdom: praying and reading.

Practically, this means asking God for wisdom each day. Like the persistent widow, we can knock on God's door every morning to simply ask, "Would You teach me to fear You and give me wisdom?" before praying for the day's concerns. Every time we meet a perplexing situation, we can look to the generous One and ask earnestly for wisdom.

It also means reading the Wisdom Books, especially the Proverbs, regularly. Don't call the support line with a question that's in the manual you never read. In the same way, if you go to the Lord asking for wisdom, make sure you're soaking up the wisdom He wrote for you.

It takes mere minutes to memorize a proverb. What a small daily investment to secure a different proverb in your head and heart each day, simply by memorizing one each morning![6] It takes a few minutes to read a chapter of the Proverbs. Read one daily, and you could complete the whole book every month. We recommend all leaders expose themselves to the Proverbs daily, however they choose to do it, and look for examples of what they've read there in real-life leadership that day.

But be warned. If you ask God for wisdom but don't actually believe that those proverbs are true and worth reading, the rest of James's words may have been written

---

6. Don't worry about review if you do this. Just try to stick with one proverb for an entire day, and then move on to another one tomorrow. You'll be surprised how often they come to mind when you need to remember them.

for you: "But let him ask in faith, with no doubting, for he who doubts is like a wave of the sea driven and tossed by the wind. For let not that man suppose that he will receive anything from the Lord; he is a double-minded man, unstable in all his ways" (James 1:6–8). If you aren't receiving God's wisdom and walking in it, it is because you lack faith in Him. You don't expect that His ways will actually help you. Do not expect to receive any wisdom from Him whose wisdom you neglect.

The Fruit of Wisdom

If wisdom comes from God into a heart that fears Him, that heart then bears fruit. The one who learns wisdom must walk in it. The heart that reveres God will hear His teaching and then "walk in the way of goodness, and keep to the paths of righteousness" (Prov. 2:20). You'll see it in a person's lifestyle. You'll also hear it in his or her voice. As wisdom pours into this heart, it will overflow with words that bring healing (12:18), speak true knowledge (15:2, 7), are well chosen and persuasive (16:23), and give life (15:4; 18:21). Wisdom is proven by the words and actions of the one who fears the Lord (Matt. 11:19; Luke 7:35; James 3:13, 17).

This is the source, heart, and fruit of heavenly wisdom. It comes from God Himself into a heart that fears Him, bearing the fruit of righteousness. This is the sort of wisdom those you lead and manage need from you. When a customer complains about an employee, that employee needs a wise manager who knows the difference between a genuine complaint and a scam. That employee will need you to remember this: "'It is good for nothing,' cries the buyer; but when he has gone his way, then he boasts" (Prov. 20:14). The public relations manager needs wisdom to see that his company's reputation—not its money—is his currency, for "a good name is to be chosen rather than great riches, loving favor rather than silver and gold" (22:1).

Everyone in leadership needs to embrace truths like, "A soft answer turns away wrath, but a harsh word stirs up anger"; and, "The plans of the diligent lead surely to plenty, but those of everyone who is hasty, surely to poverty" (Prov. 15:1; 21:5). If you want a guide through the minefield of leadership, ask God for wisdom all the time and master the Proverbs. Or, far better, let them master you.

Discussion Questions

1. Tell about a decision you had to make or a situation you had to handle that you believed you weren't wise enough to navigate.

2. How do you typically imagine God would respond to someone who lacked wisdom and asked Him for it? Does James 1:5 surprise you? Why or why not?

3. Tell about a time when you worked with a very wise or a very foolish leader. How did it affect your relationship?

4. How would you describe the connection between wisdom and the fear of the Lord?

5. How could you incorporate reading or memorizing the Proverbs into your daily life?

8 | The Allure of Counterfeit Wisdom

If there is no true wisdom without the fear of the Lord, how do godless and even strikingly wicked leaders prosper? This question has bothered God's people for a very long time (see Ps. 73:3). If I (Dave) am honest, I must admit that every time a godless opponent has risen up against me, I've felt like that person was cleverer than I was. How can godless people appear so wise if there is no fear of God before their eyes?

To this perplexing problem the Bible gives a sobering answer. There is another kind of wisdom creeping about that reaches not higher to heaven, but deeper into the pit. This is the difference James has in mind when he writes,

> Who is wise and understanding among you? Let him show by good conduct that his works are done in the meekness of wisdom. But if you have bitter envy and self-seeking in your hearts, do not boast and lie against the truth. This wisdom does not descend from above, but is earthly, sensual, demonic. For where envy and self-seeking exist, confusion and every evil thing are there. But the wisdom that is from above is first pure, then peaceable, gentle, willing to yield,

full of mercy and good fruits, without partiality and without hypocrisy. (James 3:13–17)

There is, as Paul calls it elsewhere, "the wisdom of this world" (1 Cor. 1:19–20). It is wisdom's counterfeit, her evil twin. Opposite of God-fearing wisdom, this self-exalting wisdom has a dark source, a dark heart, and dark fruit.

TWO WISDOMS

SOURCE
Satan

SOURCE
God

HEART
Advance Yourself

HEART
Fear of God

FRUIT
Conflict
Wickedness

FRUIT
Good Works
Harmony

The Heart of Counterfeit Wisdom

The dark heart of godless, counterfeit wisdom is self-worship, what James calls "envy and self-seeking." This is the desire of an individual to have the most and prove oneself the best. It lusts for honor, possessions, power, and gratification. It grabs these things apart from God, spurning God's ways, and at the expense of others. As we'll see, it can lead to some very crafty wisdom.

We might quickly think of the greedy businessman, the power-hungry ruler, and the proud Pharisee constantly scheming to stay on top and displace everyone around them. But sometimes this self-exalting wisdom shows itself not in chest-beating pride but in passionate ideology. Many of the greatest and most godless villains in history believed in what they were doing. Does their wisdom bypass the dark heart of self-exaltation? No, all these ideologies have one thing in common: they make you the hero. Once we reject the fear of God, our hearts will fashion an alternate, sometimes elaborate worldview where the one most worthy of reverence, honor, and glory is *me*.

The Source of Counterfeit Wisdom

The question that bothers so many of us is, Where do leaders like this get their apparent wisdom? If God-fearing wisdom comes from above, it is made painfully clear by James where earthly wisdom comes from. He calls it "earthly, sensual, demonic." He says it does not come from above, implying that it comes from below. The wisdom of the proud also has a person behind it, a dragon who whispers as he slithers and roars as he devours. Satan is the source of earthly wisdom.

If you deal much with snakes in real life, you know they are not always easy to see. They hide among the grass and sticks even as they slither about. Often you don't spot one until it's touching you or, worse, biting you. Hikers sometimes tell stories of brushing a fallen branch off the trail with their feet and then watching the "branch" slither away. In the same way, the ancient serpent is difficult to spot even as he is moving and working. His wisdom can be difficult to recognize even when you are handling it.

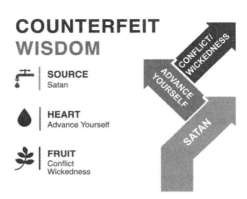

COUNTERFEIT WISDOM

SOURCE
Satan

HEART
Advance Yourself

FRUIT
Conflict
Wickedness

The Fruit of Counterfeit Wisdom

The Lord helps us here, telling us to identify Satan's "wisdom" by its fruit: "confusion and every evil thing" (James 3:16). Every other time this word for confusion is used in the Bible, it refers to conflict, sometimes even rioting or war.[1] By "every evil thing," James means all kinds of evil deeds. Self-exalting wisdom leads to conflict and all sorts of wickedness. Infighting and corruption function like the shaking tail of a rattlesnake, letting an unsuspecting person know that a venomous bite threatens. Where we see these things in boardrooms, throne rooms, and pastoral offices, we can know the place is deep in wisdom from below. If these leaders were truly "wise and understanding," their conduct would show "in the meekness of

---

1. William Arndt et al., *A Greek-English Lexicon of the New Testament and Other Early Christian Literature* (Chicago: University of Chicago Press, 2000), 35.

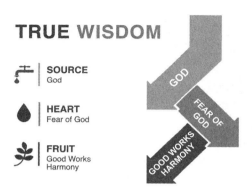

TRUE WISDOM

SOURCE
God

HEART
Fear of God

FRUIT
Good Works
Harmony

GOD
FEAR OF GOD
GOOD WORKS
HARMONY

wisdom" (3:13). We will know them by their fruits (Matt. 7:16; see also v. 20).

Living as Light in a Dark World

With this picture of Satan's darkness haunting us, we walk through a frightening world, praying we might live as agents of light. How can we lead wisely through such a perilous place?

The first thing we must do is search our hearts for these dark marks. Have our hearts ever said, "There is no God" (Ps. 14:1)? How much of our leadership comes down to being the best and having the most? What wickedness and conflict have we brought to the table?

When the Lord exposes the darkness, He is often exposing the darkness in us. So the first step is to identify our own sin and turn from it. Perhaps what you need to do is stop here, close the book, and spend time before God in confession and repentance. As you do, remember the joy of His forgiveness.

If you can come with a clear conscience, double down on your pursuit of God-fearing wisdom. The seed of the serpent has built mighty cities from Enoch (Gen. 4:17) to Babel (Gen. 11:9) to Babylon (Rev. 17:5). It is possible for the righteous to lead wisely inside them, as Daniel did in Babylon and Cornelius did in Caesarea. But it takes unusually wise and God-fearing people (Dan. 2:21, 27, 48; 4:18; Acts 10:1–2). Fighting fire with fire sounds fun, but it just burns the house down. Wise leaders must fight fire with life-giving water.

Part of this wisdom involves understanding the ways of wicked men without walking in those ways. Firefighters may put out fires, but only if they know well how fire behaves. David abhorred Saul's ways, but he knew them. Jesus reminds us to "be wise as serpents and harmless as doves" (Matt. 10:16). You will come across colorful characters in leadership, to put it kindly. Part of maintaining a commitment to righteousness is understanding their misguided ways. This never feels right, like studying a musical instrument you are forbidden to play. That is because this world is not our home. Our faithful sojourning entails godly wisdom.

The Complex World of Leadership Resources and Teaching

This brings us to one of the more amazing phenomena of the leadership world: the kaleidoscopic rabbit hole of leadership books, seminars, conferences, conversations, podcasts, and blogs that beg to be accessed. It's an expansive marketplace, filled with both heavenly and earthly wisdom. Since you will want to explore these leadership resources, you'll need discerning eyes to separate the diamonds from the dirt.

Evaluating a book, a lesson, or any teaching takes more than just considering the ideas themselves. We're right, of course, to evaluate the ideas we hear against the Bible. But often we go about this incompletely, evaluating only the propositions to be either true or false. We ask, "Is what that speaker said affirmed by the Bible or contradicted by it?" We're right about the Bible's authority over all truth when we do this, but we're thinking simplistically about how ideas work.

Wisdom is more than an idea. It's a lively seed that comes from either above or below into a heart that is either God-fearing or self-exalting and bears fruit of either righteous peace or wicked war. So when we evaluate the wisdom we're being taught, we have to look at more than just the propositions. We have to look at the source, the heart, and the fruit of the wisdom.

The easiest mark to examine is the fruit. It's easier to see bad fruit on a tree than it is to see bad roots. When you're reading a leadership book or sitting in a seminar, peer into the communities that embrace the ideas you're encountering. What sort of conduct is this wisdom producing? If the halls are filled with fighting and corruption, you already know something is wrong. As Jesus warns, beware (Matt. 7:15–20).

Though it is more difficult to see, look for selfish ambition in the heart of the teacher and the most eager students. This isn't easy, but it's possible to some degree (Prov. 20:5).

As the heart full of dark wisdom cries, "me, me, me," one can almost hear its teachers whispering, "you, you, you." What are those in the room seeking? Is the wisdom showing you how to help your team flourish or how to flourish yourself over or at the expense of your team? Often you can discern a teacher who is catering to the sinful desires, selfish ambition, and jealousy of the students. Beware.

But sometimes teachers are just submitting to how God made the world and perhaps even have some reverence for Him. From this flicker of God-fearing light can come profound principles rooted in wisdom. These teachers may not be Christians and may not even acknowledge the God who made the earth to work in such a profound way. But they at least sense that there is something in the way the world works that is worth submitting to. Sometimes they even notice something the church has missed. Discernment can reveal a heart that trembles before God, a heart with traces of the fear of God, or a heart that loves only itself.

When possible, evaluate the source of the sage's wisdom. Did the teacher learn these things from a vision they had while they were on a dream quest? Are the ideas rooted in atheism or in a strange holy book? Do they come from the semibiblical roots of Western culture? Whose voice is whispering in the teacher's ear? Zooming out to learn a writer's worldview can be enlightening, especially with ideas you know you'll be interacting with often.

You'll find a mixture of motives in almost every leadership source. The sources will be varied, the teacher's heart divided, and the fruit speckled. But at least you'll know who you're talking to. Eve would have done a better job evaluating the serpent's words if she had just admitted she was talking to a snake. Know who you're talking with, then consider what they're saying.

We can't stress enough how important it is when you consider a teacher's words to evaluate them against the Bible. If they're right, affirm it with scriptural backing. If they're unsound, don't try to defeat them with your cleverness. Counter them with the Bible or remain silent (Prov. 26:4–5). If it's a mix, seep your heart in the biblical truth near it.

Most often you'll find a mixture of all these categories. Sometimes you can cut the moldy corner off the cheese and eat the rest; sometimes the whole block is rotten and has to be thrown away. But you can't do any of this if you can't tell cheese from mold. We need heavenly wisdom so that we may practice healthy discernment.

This all, of course, comes back to true wisdom in the fear of God. Solomon saw through the schemes of a lying woman because his eyes had true wisdom. It can be frightening to consider just how deep the well of satanic wisdom goes, but leaders can do justice today if the wisdom of God is in them (see 1 Kings 3:16–28).

Discussion Questions

1. It can be perplexing to see especially wicked people prosper by the power of their own cleverness. Talk about a situation that you experienced personally or that you know about when a wicked person seemed to climb the ladder quickly.

2. Are you part of any organizations that are full of conflict and immorality? What worldly wisdom may be at the root of it?

3. Which of the principles in this chapter will help you evaluate leadership books and conferences? Of the leadership materials you've learned from so far, which do you think are more and less helpful?

9 | Zeal Flowing from God-Fearing Conviction

Effective leaders, good and evil, tend to believe in what they're doing. They hold deep convictions and speak from those beliefs in a way that moves others. This is often what we mean when we say that compelling leaders "speak from the heart." People want to follow trustworthy leaders who know what they're doing and believe in what they're doing. This chapter is about that last component—the deep convictions in a leader's heart that fill him or her with zeal and inspire others.

Something to Believe In

We're all turned off by people who don't buy what they're selling. We don't necessarily want our leaders to scream and shout, but we want to see that their hearts genuinely beat for whatever they're asking us to believe or do.

The leadership researchers we've mentioned before have varying words for this aspect of leading, from "charisma," to "motivational,"[1] to "vision."[2] One person wrote

---

1. Dorfman, Hanges, and Brodbeck, "Leadership and Cultural Variation," 673, 675, 677.

2. Bates, *Speak Like a CEO*, 208.

in a survey response, "People won't follow you, or even pay much attention to you, if you don't have any strong beliefs."[3] We use a biblical word for this: *zeal*. The people you lead want to look in your eyes and see that what you're doing together is significant. Those deep convictions, if you can learn to articulate them in a way that connects with people, can serve to hold the group together. The team will start to take seriously what you take seriously. Because they look up to you, your convictions may become their own.

This quality, more than the others we mention, tends to be what separates God-fearing leaders from other God-fearing people. Not every good person needs to be in charge of everything. But, as John Piper puts it, "God has been pleased to put a holy restlessness into some of his people, and those people will very likely be the leaders."[4]

The Bible teaches plainly that those who lead should do so with zeal (Rom. 12:8). To get an idea of what that looks like, we consider the lives of biblical leaders. They tended to fear God greatly, develop strong inward convictions from that fear, and inspire others with an outward zeal that flowed from those inward convictions.

The Certainty behind Moses's Mission

Before God called him, Moses showed more of an unholy restlessness. He saw his brothers enduring abuse and

---

3. Kouzes and Posner, *Truth about Leadership*, 43.
4. John Piper, *The Marks of a Spiritual Leader* (Minneapolis: Desiring God, 2014), 20.

burned with a discontent that led him to murder (Ex. 2:11–12). More honorably, he saw women harassed by shepherds and rescued them, eventually marrying one of them (vv. 16–22). But he would soon see something that would make him tremble with the fear of God and form him into the holy leader we know.

It started with a burning bush that was not consumed and eventually spoke the holy name "I AM." In front of this sight, Moses hid his face, filled with fear (Ex. 3:6). Trembling, Moses gained from God a clear purpose that set the course for his ministry. He would spend the rest of his life burning with God's intention "to deliver [Israel] out of the hand of the Egyptians, and to bring them up from that land to a good and large land" (v. 8). Gone was the man who took matters into his own hands, even when it meant murder. Now Moses would stand boldly before Pharaoh with one God-given purpose, dependent on God-given power. From this conviction, this certainty that God was delivering Israel, he was able to lead Israel with zeal.

In time, his fear of the Lord would grow. He would watch God's mighty hand at work through plagues in Egypt (Exodus 7–12) and miracles in the desert (e.g., Exodus 15–17). Then, strong in his trembling, he would climb the mountain and receive the law (Exodus 19–31).

God giving the law was certainly a profound experience full of the fear of the Lord. The people had to prepare themselves (Ex. 19:10–11). They couldn't even touch the mountain (v. 12). They trembled before the thundering trumpet of God's voice (v. 16). Only after God spoke would Moses be called up to receive the Ten Commandments.

And while all this was happening, the mountains "skipped like rams" (Ps. 114:6). Such a fearful encounter would lead Moses to a second deep conviction repeated throughout the rest of his ministry: the importance of obeying God's law.

Moses's sense of mission (delivering Israel) and his deepest conviction (urging Israel to obey the Lord) were forged in fiery moments full of the fear of the Lord. When he looked deep into his heart for guidance, he found only the desire to murder. When he looked trembling to the Lord, he found the focus and message of his ministry.

The Conviction behind Joshua's Courage

When we remember Joshua, we often think of a courageous warrior. Deep in his heart rested the conviction that because God was with him, Israel would inherit the promised land through his leadership. Several times we hear him encourage Israel from that very conviction. A look at his upbringing shows where that conviction was forged.

Serving as Moses's aide, Joshua would have seen many of Moses's divine encounters and mighty miracles (Num. 11:28). How many times he as a young man must have trembled while God's glory blazed, even shining from Moses's face! When the other spies quivered before the men of Canaan, he and Caleb stood firm. They did not fear their enemies because they had learned to fear the Lord.

The Lord would embolden Joshua while commissioning him to "go over this Jordan, you and all this people, to the land which I am giving to them" (Josh. 1:2). Joshua heard the voice of God say, "No man shall be able to stand before you all the days of your life" (v. 5), and "Be strong and of good courage, for to this people you shall divide as an inheritance the land which I swore to their fathers to give them" (v. 6). In such an awe-inspiring moment, Joshua would gain his own mission and have his convictional courage taken to new heights. He would charge Canaan with fervor and boldly call Israel to holiness. The conviction from which he led, then, came not from his own sense of strength but from his fear of the Lord.

The Decisive Actions of Deborah, David, and Nehemiah

Moses and Joshua received what many long for: a clear mission directly from God. Later leaders show how, even when the mission isn't spelled out in such precise detail, a high regard for the Lord often moves a leader to bold action.

One of these leaders, Deborah, served as prophetess and judge over Israel at a time when the nation was actively rejecting God as king (Judges 4–5). Two decades of oppression at the hands of the Canaanites had finally driven them to cry to the Lord for rescue (Judg. 4:3). The people were already looking to her for leadership (vv. 4–10). As she looked at them, she saw no one taking action. When she delivered God's call to Barak, even he hesitated (vv. 6–9, 14). So she "arose a mother in Israel" to lead them (5:7). She did this without knowing all the specifics of what would happen. Her courage would inspire Barak, Jael, and many others to display bravery of their own.

Ultimately, Sisera, the king of Canaan, was killed at the hands of Jael, and the people were free—in large part thanks to Deborah's zeal (Judg. 4:17–24). After this decisive victory, the celebratory "Song of Deborah and Barak" expresses her desire:

> When leaders lead in Israel,
> When the people willingly offer themselves,
> Bless the LORD! (5:2)

Her relationship with the Lord moved her to act boldly for the Lord.

As Deborah arose when no one else would, David stared down a giant when no one else would. With fire in his eyes, he spoke words that inspired Israel, showed his conviction, and indicated the source of his conviction. He said boldly, "Who is this uncircumcised Philistine, that he should defy the armies of the living God?" (1 Sam. 17:26). Those words inspired Israel. They caused such a stir that they were quickly passed from the lips of this obscure shepherd boy all the way to King Saul (v. 31). The words themselves show their source: his high esteem for God's name.

We never read of God explicitly commanding David to go and fight Goliath. Yet David knew he must do it. He knew the Philistine could not live after mocking the army whose God was the Lord. He knew that as God's anointed, it fell on him to do the business. Here we see the way contagious convictions work for most Christian leaders, who do not get prophetic instructions on what to do today. Because David feared God, he had strong convictions about the way God fights for His people. He also held strong convictions about his duty as God's anointed. With that conviction formed over years, he instinctually knew what he must do when the moment came. This is the way of a man after God's own heart (see 1 Sam. 13:14).

Like David in his courageous move to confront Goliath, Nehemiah was not given an explicit word on Jerusalem's broken walls—only a deep conviction and an opportunity to act on it. An Israelite exile raised in a God-fearing home would have sung often of God's love for Jerusalem's wall and gates (Ps. 87:2). For Nehemiah and his peers, fearing God meant sharing His love for Jerusalem and living faithfully while kept far outside the gates.

This deep reverence and closeness to God's heart helps us to understand Nehemiah's emotional reaction to the report: "The wall of Jerusalem is also broken down, and its gates are burned with fire" (Neh. 1:3). Only one with a deep love for God would weep for days over walls that were hundreds of miles away he had probably never seen. He prays a prayer rooted in the fear of the "great and awesome God" (v. 5), full of confession and an unwavering faith in God's promises. He even mentions those "who desire to fear Your name" (v. 11).[5]

At the end of his prayer, Nehemiah asks God for a chance to fix the walls. But he never acts with entitlement, presuming that God must honor his request. He waits four months before God moves the heart of the king in his favor. But once Nehemiah gets to speak, his words show his love for the wall and the people of Israel. He is bold enough to ask if he can rebuild the wall.

---

5. See also Neh. 5:15 and 7:2, where both Nehemiah and Hananiah are said to fear God.

Later, when Nehemiah confronts corruption in Jerusalem, the fear of God again becomes the core of his
contagious conviction. He tells the wicked officials, "What
you are doing is not good. Should you not walk in the fear
of our God because of the reproach of the nations, our
enemies?" (Neh. 5:9). They listened, even swearing before
the priests that they would restore what they took. We see
the pattern again here. Because he feared God, he had a
strong conviction for justice. Then when he saw injustice,
his love for God overflowed through inspiring words.

The Ardent Faith of Mary Magdalene, Peter, and Paul

The pattern of awe leading to convictional action continues throughout the New Testament. For example, in His
postresurrection appearance to Mary Magdalene, Jesus
reveals His identity first by calling her by name (John
20:16). He then moves her from a literal posture of fearful love and worship (clinging to Him) to a mission of
pivotal proclamation (running to tell the others). "With
fear and great joy" (Matt. 28:8), she was to go and tell the
other disciples that she had seen Jesus resurrected (John
20:17–18).[6] Peter heard her startling account. While the
other disciples took the story as "idle tales," he and John
rushed to see the empty tomb. He was awestruck and
"marveling to himself at what had happened" (Luke 24:11–
12). That moment proved essential to Peter's formation
and passion as a fisher of men and a shepherd to Jesus's
sheep. That passion was developed by the Lord Himself

---

6. Luke's account notes that other women were present (see 24:10).

during awe-filled moments by the sea (Matt. 4:18–22; John 21:15–19). Even Peter's letters flow with this contagious conviction for evangelism and shepherding (1 Peter 2:11–12; 5:1–5).

Similarly, the apostle Paul's preaching and letters burned with a passion to reach the Gentiles (Eph. 3:8), a mission given to him shortly after his fearsome encounter on the road to Damascus (Acts 9:15–19). Like Moses and Joshua, these New Testament leaders' missions were more explicit. Like all the leaders we've surveyed here, the passions from which they inspired others flowed from their view of God.

Conviction for Christian Leaders Today

It could be tragic to miss the dark antithesis of this pattern, clearly seen in the story of Babel. As the people built their offensive tower, destined to fall, the place buzzed with a very different but contagious conviction: "Let us make a name for ourselves" (Gen. 11:4). Without regard for God's name, their own name and glory became central. A conviction like this can be even more contagious. As the old line goes, "Pride and vanity have built more hospitals than all the virtues together."[7] At Babel we find a warning: self-exalting convictions are effective but ill-fated.

As Christian leaders today put to death impulses to exalt self, we may follow in the footsteps of heroes like Joshua and Peter. We build our convictions on the same

---

7. Bernard de Mandeville, *The Fable of the Bees* (London: T. Ostell, 1806), 353.

foundation they did. It helps to see this process of God-fearing, convictional leadership as beginning in the fear of God, leading to the convictions built on that fear, which enables us to develop the skill of stating those convictions in a way that resonates with people.

First, as you grow in the fear of God, let it form your deepest values. With every sermon you hear, learn to love what God loves. In every wise old man's words, learn what values last a lifetime. When you're reading your Bible, stop to worship the Lord and take note of what is important to Him. Eventually, you'll become a person who, after God's own heart, has had convictions forged in the furnace of the fear of the Lord. Then, perhaps when you don't expect it, a moment may come when those convictions force you to say, "I know what I must do."

This is such a better way to find a calling than the exhausting self-examination young leaders are often pushed toward. When we search our hearts for clues to our destiny, we find only deceit and wickedness. How miserable! At best, we deceive ourselves. At worst, we become absorbed with ourselves. But happiness is never found by staring into ourselves; it is only discovered when we behold God. Yes, let trusted friends help you understand your strengths and weaknesses. And hold them both in humility. But when it comes to the passions that keep you going, let them be found when looking upward, not inward.

Then, to lead others, develop the skill of communicating those convictions well. Some mild-mannered leaders need to learn how to let their passion come through in their tone and body language. Others may need to tone it down so they can be taken more seriously. This isn't about finding the best zinger or learning to perform, but about making sure God's heart, your heart, your voice, and your body language align.

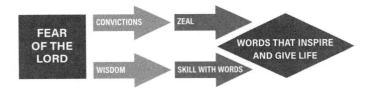

If you're in a leadership position, it helps to regularly evaluate your message and all your communication outlets. What are the main convictions you're operating from right now? How biblical are they? Once you've reviewed these beliefs, consider all the ways you are communicating, or could be communicating, with the people you lead. Are you using them all wisely and effectively? Everything—from meetings to phone calls, to sermons, to emails—is an opportunity to make those God-fearing convictions evident. If they are formed by God and founded in His Word, wear them on your sleeve.

As you communicate these convictions, learn to communicate with the beauty, clarity, depth, and variety we find in our Bibles. A lover of the Bible will soon become a lover of song; story; short, memorable proverbs; pastoral letters; biography; and concrete images. Top-level for-profit and nonprofit business leaders tend to be skilled storytellers. A wise leader will take the time to think of a few stories that communicate a conviction and then work to tell those stories well and often. A pastor who can sense God's desire for his church to grow in compassion may want to add a few songs about compassion into Sunday gatherings. There is wisdom in stating core values in short, memorable proverbs that a leader can repeat and reinforce. All the types of communication in the Bible are useful to the King, so they are useful for our leadership as well. However you state them, these values must flow downriver from the high throne of God into a leader's heart and mind. This God-centered conduit safeguards leaders from straying outside of His Word and is also the most effective way to maintain their gospel motivation and love for Christ.

Discussion Questions

1. Tell about a time when you worked with a leader who didn't seem to care about the work you were doing together.

2. What are your favorite stories of zealous biblical leaders who believed in what they were doing?

3. Think about some of the happiest moments of your life. Did they occur when you were looking at yourself, or when you were consumed by something outside yourself? What does that say about the world's advice to look within yourself for happiness and guidance?

4. As you've grown closer to Jesus, what deepening convictions have you begun to develop?

5. If you serve in leadership, what would you say are the core convictions that guide you and your team? How could you better communicate strong convictions that help keep everyone aligned?

10 | **God-Fearing Leadership and the Family**

As people thought in the past, many today believe there is a connection between strong families and upright leaders. Often they view people with a strong family life as trustworthy, knowing and believing in what they're doing. A leader's relationships are built on trust and credibility, and having a strong family gives the sense that a leader has a certain measure of both. This holds true even as Western culture loses its sense of certainty about what a family is. Regardless of their beliefs about the nature of family, people have it written on their hearts to cherish a noble mother and a dedicated father.

God is the one who imprinted that desire on our hearts. If He blesses a leader with a family, he expects that person to lead his family well. Pastors in the church need a track record of good family leadership shown by marital fidelity and the conduct of their children.[1] Paul says it more explicitly than most people would say it today: if a

---

1. A thorough encouragement to single pastors is outside the bounds of this chapter, but we urge unmarried pastors to live with an evident and holy chastity that displays the supreme worth of Jesus.

man can't lead his own home, how can he lead the church (1 Tim. 3:2, 4–5; Titus 1:6)?

This expectation was strong in the Old Testament as well. When Moses failed to circumcise his son, the Lord tolerated this disobedience for years. But then He commissioned Moses to lead Israel, and only days later He sought to put him to death over that sin (Ex. 4:24–26). As a positive example, Joshua exhorted Israel not only with his own faithfulness but with his family's faithfulness (Josh. 24:15). David's and Solomon's poor family leadership are treated as major failures.[2]

While God's expectation is consistent, He gave us more than commands and examples. He also shows us what this expectation is built on.

For the wife:

Charm is deceitful and beauty is passing,
But a woman who fears the LORD, she shall be
     praised. (Prov. 31:30)

For the husband:

Your wife shall be like a fruitful vine
In the very heart of your house,
Your children like olive plants
All around your table.
Behold, thus shall the man be blessed
Who fears the LORD. (Ps. 128:3–4)

The cherished wife of Proverbs 31 has many admirable qualities, which crescendo at the summary, "a woman who

---

2. For example, see 1 Kings 11, where Solomon's downfall stems from his many marriages.

fears the LORD." All her excellence is captured in this trait. The man who sees his family flourish under his care is the man "who fears the LORD." For both the husband and wife, family leadership is grounded in the fear of the Lord.

To be sure, these passages can be taken too far if Christians misunderstand them. In them we see God's covenant promises to Israel to prosper the families of Israelites who feared Him. We see a window into God's heart, how He enjoys blessing those who fear Him. And we see a picture of God's wisdom, how God-fearing wisdom brings practical blessings to a family.

Covenant Promises: Fear God and Flourish

Israel heard these words as God's covenant nation. Unlike the nations around them, they could call Him by His covenant name, the Lord. God had made a covenant with them on the mountain of the Lord, which we can read in the books of Exodus, Leviticus, and Deuteronomy. The basic idea was, "Fear Me, keep My ways, and I will bless you beyond measure; worship other gods, forsake My ways, and I will punish you terribly."

For Israelites who feared God, one of those promised blessings was abundant fertility. They could expect to see their children multiply, their fields produce, their spinning wheel spin, and their business deals profit. This would create no small amount of work. But the God-fearing husband and wife would meet that work with wise diligence. Thus, the God-fearing wife rises early to set food on a large table and buy another field (Prov. 31:15–16). God's people could expect these blessings because His covenant promised them to those who feared Him and kept His ways.

In the death and resurrection of Jesus Christ, this covenant was finally and forever fulfilled. Jesus feared God and walked in all His ways, yet He endured the terrible punishment of those who sin against God. Those who have not feared God or walked in His ways yet trust in Jesus are given the eternal life and abundance that Jesus established. This fulfills the old covenant and inaugurates a new and better one.

Where the ancient Israelites' covenant promised *temporary* life and flourishing, our covenant promises *eternal* life and flourishing. Eternal flourishing in a new earth is better than an abundant field today. But—and here is the important part—while Israel's obedience to the covenant was fulfilled with temporal prosperity, a godly couple today may suffer infertility, hunger, or persecution. A godly spouse may be abandoned. The promise God's people cling to now is that none of these problems can separate them from the love of God or the abundance that is to come (Rom. 8:35).[3]

So Christians cannot treat the promises of Psalm 128 and Proverbs 31 as a personal guarantee because Israel's covenant has been fulfilled in Jesus's death and resurrection. This would be like expecting a widow to maintain her marriage vows even though her covenant was fulfilled

---

3. For insight on the covenant structure of the Old and New Testaments, see Peter J. Gentry and Stephen J. Wellum, *God's Kingdom through God's Covenants: A Concise Biblical Theology* (Wheaton, Ill.: Crossway, 2015).

when her husband died (Rom. 7:2–6). Today, fearing God does not guarantee a good family life.

God's Heart and Wisdom on Display

Still, a Christian has much to gain from understanding these two passages. In them we see God's delight in strong families and the wisdom that tends to form them.

God's covenant with Israel teaches us much about His heart when we remember that He chose every detail of the covenant Himself. This holy treaty was not negotiated by God and Moses. It was handed down from God to Moses. As we read the law and see it meditated on in the Psalms and Proverbs, we should ask often, What does this say about God's heart?

Since God didn't have to make any of these promises, what does it say about Him that He chose to? What does it say that He would make flourishing homes led by a God-fearing husband and wife a necessary element in His covenant intentions? It shows us that He delights in these families. He made the promise, laid out the path, and even told the people to teach it to their children, all with the desire of seeing homes thrive in the fear of the Lord. This is a God who loves a busy, growing, bustling house under the rule of a God-fearing man and woman.

This has been His heart from the beginning, when He blessed the first man and woman saying that they should "be fruitful and multiply" (Gen. 1:28). God's desire is that there be godly children raised by a godly man and woman (Mal. 2:15). We should see His delight in the spinning wheel of Proverbs 31 and the crowded table of Psalm 128. If God desires strong homes like these, we should desire them too.

Because these passages reside in the Wisdom Literature, we should look to them for wisdom. A God-fearing man or woman may not be guaranteed a strong family, but his or her wisdom and integrity make a strong family more likely. God-fearing leadership blesses homes the same way it blesses other institutions: by providing leaders with integrity, wisdom, and convictions while creating a just environment.

A husband and wife who tremble before God will embrace His design for marriage. They will learn to delight in a one-man and one-woman union, refusing to share their bed with others. They will learn to model Christ and the church through sacrificial leadership and willful submission. They will learn to see children as a blessing, even while they change diaper after diaper. They will discipline and train their children in the Lord's ways. Principles like these aren't arbitrary; they actually work. Those who fear the Lord learn His ways, and His ways tend to strengthen families.

Not only do God-fearing couples learn His ways, but they gain the integrity to walk in them. It takes wisdom to know that flirting with another woman is a bad idea; it takes integrity to keep from doing it when temptation strikes. It takes wisdom to believe that children need to be disciplined; it takes integrity to get up off the couch and do it again. The fear of the Lord leads to both.

The fear of the Lord produces convictions that become bedrock for parents. It moves them to see children as a blessing and parenting as a God-commissioned task. This sobers new parents and leads them to think, "With God's help I will give this all I have." It encourages a sleepless mother whose only moment to read her Bible comes while nursing her child in the middle of the night. Convictions forged in the fear of the Lord have the strength to last through the challenges of pregnancy, overflowing diaper pails, school bullies, rebellious teenagers, and college sendoffs. In turn, children are blessed. Children simply do better when, through good and bad, their parents see them as blessings and take parenting them seriously.

The fear of the Lord also upholds justice in a home. Parents often must judge their children's disputes. If they remember, "I will answer to God for how I use my power here," they are motivated to stop what they are doing, learn the truth, and decide fairly. This leads to the sort of home where children are safer, where they cannot manipulate their parents or each other very easily. Because parents chase wickedness out of the house, children grow up healthier.

All of this sounds abhorrent to those who are wise in their own eyes. How tempting it is to craft our own goals for marriage, to piece together principles for how to get there, even to define it our way. Those with a high regard for God want nothing of this; admit in humility, "I don't know how to do this"; and look to God for help. How blessed a treasure they will find, for the Lord's ways are good.

To those who fear Him, God gives wisdom and ideals that tend to form strong families. So a family can be a test of leadership ability, especially for a father. The same foundation that made him a good father may also make him a good leader outside his home. Worldly people, with God's designs written on their hearts, know something of this.

This is why even people who abhor Christian family values still admire a "family man."

The takeaway, then, is this: If God gives you a wife or husband, love her or him in the fear of the Lord. If He gives you children, train them in the fear of the Lord. Take the principles of family you were taught and say to the Lord, "These are nothing without Your help; teach me Your ways." Sit at His feet with His Word open and learn His ways. On this foundation, God will form you into a better spouse, parent, and leader.

Discussion Questions

1. Do you find it easier to trust a leader who is also a good mother or father? How does that change how you look at her or him?

2. How do the principles in this chapter help guard us against the prosperity gospel—the idea that God rewards faithfulness with health and wealth?

3. If you are married or have children, talk about any proverb or psalm that has given you help in marriage or parenting.

4. Explain how the fear of God can make someone a better spouse and parent.

5. How could the principles in this chapter help a single person?

11 | The Leader and God-Fearing Justice

A friend of mine (Dave) tells the story of working for a small business and being disappointed in her boss, who had fired a receptionist. The receptionist didn't work very hard and didn't seem concerned about her mistakes, but she needed the money. My friend's heart broke for the receptionist, and she wondered how her boss could be so insensitive.

A few years later, she bought the business from her boss. She says her eyes were opened when she found herself in the same position. Another employee wasn't showing up, didn't work hard when he did show up, and was causing problems that affected customers and other employees. She felt compassion for this employee too. But this time she saw that if she didn't take action, business would drop off and all the employees would suffer. Her team looked to her to make the difficult but right decision, for their good.

With authority come difficult situations like these. To handle them well, in a way that pleases God and benefits the whole group, we have to look to God for help in leading justly. The Bible consistently describes God-fearing leaders as just. Yet as the world becomes more uncertain about God and His ways, its concept of justice becomes equally uncertain. At the same time, our understanding of biblical justice has been muddied by those who once distorted the Bible's teaching to promote injustices like slave trade or those today who similarly twist the Scriptures to excuse domestic abuse.

Clearing up this confusion, the Bible paints a refreshing picture of justice and urges leaders to act accordingly. This chapter is about the Bible's understanding of justice, the connection of justice with the fear of God, and its way of making groups of people flourish.

Just Living

As we've written before, a person who trembles before God begins to see how good His ways are. No longer are we right in our own eyes, defining right and wrong as we please. No longer do we start with an ideology and fashion a god around it. We bring our measure for right and wrong into alignment with God's standard. As much as we place ourselves under God's morals and live within them, we are living just, righteous lives.

For everyday living, justice is doing to others what God says is right and not doing to others what God says is wrong. Put another way, it's doing the right thing in daily life. When left alone with someone else's wallet, a just person doesn't steal the money in it. When the boss is in a meeting off-site, a just employee still performs her job well. Even though Joseph thought Mary had been unfaithful to him, he sought to end the engagement in a way that wouldn't bring shame on her (Matt. 1:19). The Bible uses words like *just* and *righteous* interchangeably to describe people like this.

Because true definitions of *right* and *wrong* come from God's character and His Word, only a person who takes God and His Word seriously can live a truly just life. That is why when the Bible reveals God's expectation for people, it says they are to "fear God and keep His commandments," or, in another place, to fear God and do "what is right" (Eccl. 12:13; Acts 10:35 ESV). Following God's commandments and doing what is right are the same thing, and both come from fearing God.

By contrast, those who do not take God seriously will not take His ways seriously. Wise in their own eyes, they will inevitably stray from God's ways into an unjust life.

Just Leadership

Since all people must fear God and do the right thing, those in authority have yet another sobering responsibility. It isn't enough for people in charge to live moral lives themselves. Just leaders have to act as God's judge over other people's rights and wrongs. "While we may identify leadership with prestige and elite standing, the Bible generally commends leadership as a way to pursue justice."[1] For a person trusted with authority, pursuing justice means rewarding what God says is right and punishing what God says is wrong. Parents cannot let their children do whatever they want. They are called to discipline their children in God's ways. Police officers are called to both protect us and write us tickets when we drive too fast. Teachers are

---

1. Arthur Boers, *Servants and Fools: A Biblical Theology of Leadership* (Nashville: Abingdon, 2015), 96.

called to reward the students when they follow the rules and punish them when they bully each other. After my friend bought the business, she had to reward employees when they did well and—yes—she did fire that worker.[2]

For governments, this justice is mostly established and maintained by writing and enforcing laws (the latter often done by a judge or a justice). Martin Luther King Jr. defined *justice* with his trademark poetic clarity: "A just law is a man-made code that squares with the moral law or the law of God. An unjust law is a code that is out of harmony with the moral law."[3] The more these laws are written to reflect the character and ways of God and the more they are enforced fairly, the more just the environment should be.

Some leaders are also stewarded with cultural influence. For them, a just society is important. Members of a just society not only keep just laws but order their relationships by God's design, treat each other according to God's ways, and celebrate together what God calls good. A just society has just relationships, expects just norms, and creates just art. A society known for the way husbands considerately and steadily lead their wives is just. A society where voters curse government leaders they do not support is unjust. Twitter hashtags that celebrate generosity are socially just. A movie director who makes films that glorify immorality is promoting social injustice.

Like the rest of us, leaders do not have the authority

---

2. A few details about this story are changed for the sake of anonymity.

3. Martin Luther King Jr., "Letter from the Birmingham Jail," as quoted in Ken Magnuson, *Invitation to Christian Ethics: Moral Reasoning and Contemporary Issues* (Grand Rapids: Kregel Academic, 2020), 476.

to determine what is right and wrong based on their self-defined standards. Instead, they have the authority to reward what God deems right and punish what God says is wrong.[4] Cultural influencers have the commission only to celebrate what God says is right and steer people away from what God says is wrong. Just leadership, then, comes from fearing the God who declares right from wrong. If we are wise in our own eyes, we'll define right and wrong for ourselves, write the rules poorly, and enforce them unfairly.

So a just society is one in which individuals live under God's ways, relationships are ordered along God's ways, culture celebrates what God calls good, and the recognized laws square with God's laws.

This is why, as Israel drifted from obedience to God, they drifted from justice. The prophet Isaiah rose to confront them:

> But your iniquities have separated you from
>   your God;
> And your sins have hidden His face from you,
> So that He will not hear. (Isa. 59:2)

And shortly afterward he declares,

> Therefore justice is far from us,
> Nor does righteousness overtake us. (v. 9)

Because Israel was far from God and walking in sin, justice eluded them. It only comes when a people, especially their leaders, regard the Lord highly enough to listen to His ways.

---

4. Magnuson, *Invitation to Christian Ethics*, 402.

Two Marks of Justice: Impartiality and Wisdom

When God wrote Israel's laws, His care for the powerless was evident. He wrote specific laws to protect travelers passing through who had almost no social rights (Ex. 22:21; 23:9; Lev. 19:10, 33–34; 23:22; Deut. 10:19; 14:29). He required Israel to care for the poor (Lev. 25:35; Deut. 10:18; 24:14). He regulated slavery and made man-stealing a capital offense to protect the poor (Ex. 21:16). He did not want the powerful oppressing the weak.

He also demanded that Israel enforce this law fairly, without partiality. Judges were instructed, "You shall not show partiality in judgment; you shall hear the small as well as the great" (Deut. 1:17; see also Lev. 19:15; Deut. 16:19; Prov. 24:23; 28:21). These judges had to be "men, such as fear God, men of truth, hating covetousness" (Ex. 18:21). We tend to favor people who are like us and who can help us out later, which is why bribery and prejudice have long and terrible histories. But everyone was to get an equal hearing before God's bench. In a decision between the rich man with a gift and the poor man with evidence, justice chose the poor man with evidence.

God requires this impartiality from all leaders (Gal. 2:6; Eph. 6:9; 1 Tim. 5:21; James 2:1). Parents cannot hold a favored child to an easier standard. Pastors cannot give special treatment to members who can give more money. Police officers cannot mistreat suspects who don't look like them. Bosses can't hold the employees they like and the employees they don't like to two different standards.

This is because the God we fear is impartial (Deut. 10:17; 1 Peter 1:17). When He comes to judge us, He will not be impressed with our wealth, our social class, the group we identify with, or the nation we come from. We will be judged only by whether we have feared Him and done what is right (Acts 10:34–35; see also Job 32:21; Rom. 2:11; Col. 3:25). In line with His impartial character, just leadership hears each person equally and judges each person based on what he or she has done.

As well as revering God's ways and imitating His impartiality, another hallmark of just leadership is God's wisdom. Two women came before Solomon, both claiming to be the mother of the same child and demanding that the child be sent home with them. The king asked for a sword to divide the child between them, knowing that the boy's true mother would never allow it. When one of them cried, "O my lord, give her the living child, and by no means kill him!" Solomon knew that she was the mother (1 Kings 3:26). This was all a display of the wonderful wisdom God had given to him. The reason the people stood in awe of him was because "they saw that the wisdom of God was in him to administer justice" (v. 28).

Leadership is fraught with sticky situations like this, conundrums that require wisdom to discern the just action and outcome. A leader must learn how to seek and evaluate information, how to discern the truth and spot a lie. Parents must learn how to ask their children the right questions and determine who really hit whom. Judges must learn to weigh evidence and see through shady advocates. Questions about what really happened and what is the right thing to do aren't always easy to answer. Exploring them requires wisdom.[5]

We don't have the wisdom to do justice, and we do not see everything. So God-fearing leaders must look to God for wisdom and wait for God's justice when they cannot see what really happened (Prov. 2:6–11; 28:5).

A Just Environment Brings Flourishing

When governor, parent, or boss rises with wisdom to impartially reward what God calls good and punish what God calls evil, an environment is created where people can flourish (Prov. 20:26; 21:15; 29:4). Earlier, we explored King David's picture of leadership that brings health. The idea was that God-fearing leaders give life to a group like the sun gives life to wet grass. That is, they create the conditions for it to grow.

Now is the time to mention the other half of this God-fearing rule: justice. David says,

> He who rules over men must be just,
> Ruling in the fear of God.
> And he shall be like the light of the morning when
> the sun rises,
> A morning without clouds,
> Like the tender grass springing out of the earth,
> By clear shining after rain. (2 Sam. 23:3–4)

People were made to flourish under God's just rule. It follows, then, that a leader who introduces God's just ways to

---

5. The Proverbs make a strong connection between wisdom and justice in 1:3; 8:20; 17:23; 21:3, 15.

a group will also bring health to that group. He is setting up an environment where people become their best and benefit the most.

When a sports league has a good rulebook and matches are overseen by wise, impartial umpires, the whole league benefits. The athletes will be safer and the games more fun to watch or play.

When a CEO establishes sound rules and enforces them fairly, the whole company benefits. Employees won't fear being mistreated by their coworkers. They'll do better work knowing that they will be held accountable and that their coworkers are more likely to follow through. Customers are better served, bringing back more return business, and the company's reputation improves.

When cultural influencers create taglines, hashtags, songs, and movies that celebrate godly fathers, fair treatment of the powerless, diligent work, and the beauty of the Milky Way, society changes for the better. Children grow up under better fathers. The powerless get treated more fairly. People benefit from the diligent work of others. And stargazers stop more often to look up.

When parents follow God's ways and discipline their children in them, the whole home is blessed. Sisters don't have to be afraid of what their brother will do to them. Everyone learns good habits. This safe, godly environment is the sort of place where children can slowly grow into healthy adults.

When the government and police can enforce true justice in a neighborhood, the people who live and work there can become more financially secure. Residents can do business without fear of theft or vandalism. Jobs are created. Fewer people suffer violence. Property values rise. Education becomes more accessible.

If God has given you leadership over a group, He calls you to fear Him and represent Him justly. When your craft influences others, point them in the right direction. When you get to write the rules, write them according to God's ways. When you have to enforce them, reward what God calls good and punish what He calls evil. Do it impartially and seek God's wisdom. These are the conditions under which the people you lead can flourish.

Discussion Questions

1. Tell about a time in leadership when the right decision was a hard one, like the decision of Dave's friend to fire an ineffective worker.

2. How would you describe what just living and just leadership look like?

3. Where you live, what are the current political issues people talk about? How would a biblical understanding of justice inform those issues?

4. Have you ever worked with a leader who was especially just or unjust? What was that situation like?

12 | The Undeniable Cost of God-Fearing Leadership

As Christians fear and follow the Suffering Servant, they become like Him. This sounds exciting until we remember that following Him leads to suffering and servitude. Living and leading in the fear of the Lord is a blessed way to spend your life, but it comes with a high cost. This final chapter is about that cost—the deep, personal cost of following Jesus while you lead others.

Jesus's sobering words "Whoever desires to become great among you, let him be your servant. And whoever desires to be first among you, let him be your slave" were spoken to twelve men and one woman who were ambitious to lead (Matt. 20:26–27). These words are even more applicable to ambitious leaders than to other Christians. Those who follow Jesus, especially those who follow Him into leadership, follow Him into service and suffering.

There is hardly a Christian leader who does not value the term *servant leader*. Probably because of Jesus's words, a movement of servant leadership continues to grow within the church and among others influenced by the Judeo-Christian ethic. The movement originated with the ideas of Robert Greenleaf, who retired from AT&T and, beginning in 1970, taught that a leader's ambitions should come from a desire to serve others.[1]

It's easy to see that Greenleaf's idea has been a refreshing step in the right direction and why it's still popular today. But critics have a strong comeback: What exactly does *servant leader* mean? It's easier to trumpet the value of a leader who serves others but harder to agree on what that would look like. Do servant leaders lead authoritatively for the good of others? Work with their hands as much as with their words? Obey the voice of the people, like a servant? Give the corner office to an intern?[2]

For leaders who sit at the feet of Jesus, His words give a powerful answer: "Whoever desires to be first among you, let him be your slave—*just as the Son of Man* did not come to be served, but to serve, and to give His life a ransom for many" (Matt. 20:27–28). We should serve the same way Jesus served.

The Bible expressly calls Jesus a servant in two other prominent places: Philippians 2 and Isaiah 52. If we are going to serve like Him, these two pictures show us what it may look like. In Philippians 2, the apostle Paul explains that Jesus took on the form of a servant by humbling Himself. Jesus, "being in the form of God, did not consider

---

1. Don M. Frick, "Robert K. Greenleaf: A Short Biography," Greenleaf Center for Servant Leadership, https://www.greenleaf.org/about-us/robert-k-greenleaf-biography/.

2. See Northouse, *Leadership: Theory and Practice*, 230, 241, for a comparison of several expert takes on the concept and other criticisms of the movement, including the lack of consensus on the meaning of *servant leadership*.

it robbery to be equal with God, but made Himself of no reputation, taking the form of a bondservant, and coming in the likeness of men" (vv. 6–7). Though He was God, He took on a human body with all its infections, pulled muscles, and other weaknesses. In this way He humbled Himself to things far below His dignity for the sake of others.

Following Jesus, then, must mean humbling ourselves to things that are (or seem) far beneath us. The pastor of a thriving church plant shouldn't look down his nose when it's time to set up chairs. A manager at a restaurant shouldn't shiver at the dripping trash bags and leave them for the dish crew to throw away. A Christian leader should often hear, "You shouldn't have to do that."

Humbling ourselves is hard, but Jesus's servanthood goes even deeper. Isaiah's Suffering Servant endured humiliation from others and suffered oppression for the sake of His own:

> Behold, My Servant shall deal prudently;
> He shall be exalted and extolled and be very high.
> Just as many were astonished at you,
> So His visage was marred more than any man,
> And His form more than the sons of men.
>   (Isa. 52:13–14)

> He is despised and rejected by men,
> A Man of sorrows and acquainted with grief.
> And we hid, as it were, our faces from Him;
> He was despised, and we did not esteem Him. (53:3)

Jesus didn't take on a lower position just for Himself; He let others esteem Him as lowly. He humbled Himself to take on a human body and then allowed others to beat that body so grotesquely that it no longer looked human. He didn't respond when they blindfolded Him, struck Him, and mocked, "Prophesy! Who is the one who struck You?" (Luke 22:64). He endured when the crowd around Him and the thieves beside Him taunted Him and demanded that He prove Himself by coming down from the cross (Matt. 27:40–42; Mark 15:30–32).

This is the difference between humbling yourself and being humiliated by others; the difference between admitting, "I'm not the greatest teacher in the world" and hearing your students respond, "You sure aren't." Often Jesus calls His followers to cross this line with Him for the sake of others. He called white civil rights protesters to endure taunting for marching with black brothers and sisters. Today He calls some pastors to endure hatred for proclaiming a Christian sexual ethic. He has long called mothers to lovingly discipline their disrespectful children rather than fuming or sulking. These Christians are true students of their Teacher, who was exalted higher than they will ever be exalted but was despised more than they will ever be despised.

The Song of the Suffering Servant also points beyond humiliation to Jesus's physical suffering:

> He was oppressed and He was afflicted,
> Yet He opened not His mouth;
> He was led as a lamb to the slaughter,
> And as a sheep before its shearers is silent,
> So He opened not His mouth.
> He was taken from prison and from judgment,
> And who will declare His generation?
> For He was cut off from the land of the living;

For the transgressions of My people He was stricken.
And they made His grave with the wicked—
But with the rich at His death,
Because He had done no violence,
Nor was any deceit in His mouth. (Isa. 53:7–9)

The fulfillment of these words was experienced in the span of a single day. Roman soldiers used a scourge to shred Jesus's back and then forced a crown of thorns onto His head (John 19:1–2). They brutally fastened Him to a cross to bleed and suffocate to death (v. 18).

Sometimes the conflicts and persecution that come with Christian leadership stop at mockery and derision, but other times they turn violent. Terrorist groups behead missionaries and post the videos on the internet. Principals absorb bullets meant for students. Leaders who bring change to organizations often pay with bodily ailments, sometimes a personal cost of the stress they've endured. Leaders who follow Jesus must wake up every morning ready to sacrifice and even die for the people they lead.

Jesus also suffered for others in ways not explicitly connected with His servanthood. His heart ached at the betrayal of a close confidant (Matt. 26:46) and at the abandonment of friends (vv. 69–76). He wept over a city that would not follow Him (23:37–39). He repeatedly endured disciples who didn't understand His teaching (Matt. 15:16; 16:11; Mark 4:13; 6:52; 7:18; 8:17–21; 9:32; Luke 9:45; John 8:27; 12:16; 20:9). Those who lead under Him can relate.

Serving like Jesus, then, means humbling yourself, being humiliated by others, and enduring physical suffering. Another way we see this is in the timing of Jesus's words.

The scene was heavy and dark because Jesus had just told the disciples for the third time of the suffering that awaited Him at the end of their climb. Once they arrived at Jerusalem and celebrated the Passover together, the Song of the Suffering Servant would be fulfilled in His arrest, suffering, and death: "Behold, we are going up to Jerusalem, and the Son of Man will be betrayed to the chief priests and to the scribes; and they will condemn Him to death, and deliver Him to the Gentiles to mock and to scourge and to crucify. And the third day He will rise again" (Matt. 20:18–19). One reason Jesus says this when He does, the reason that Matthew includes it here, is to make the next words sound as shockingly out of place as they are.

> Then the mother of Zebedee's sons came to Him with her sons, kneeling down and asking something from Him.
> And He said to her, "What do you wish?"
> She said to Him, "Grant that these two sons of mine may sit, one on Your right hand and the other on the left, in Your kingdom." (vv. 20–21)

Into the dark clouds of Jesus's grim prediction, the mother's ambition arrives with all the tact of a foghorn. This is no time to present a stage-mother campaign to the Son of Man.

She has a motive. In the first century, she can only find power if her sons find power. She knows this, so she tries to elevate herself by elevating them. The sons play along. The disciples get angry. Seeing the conflict, Jesus quells things down by saying,

You know that the rulers of the Gentiles lord it over them, and those who are great exercise authority over them. Yet it shall not be so among you; but whoever desires to become great among you, let him be your servant. And whoever desires to be first among you, let him be your slave—just as the Son of Man did not come to be served, but to serve, and to give His life a ransom for many. (vv. 25–28)

All this means that Jesus spoke these famous words against our natural desire to be served. The mother, the sons, and the other ten disciples have shown their cards; they all want power. They'll ask for it, fight for it, fume over it—whatever it takes. Jesus says the world around them works the same way. Unions, managers, and executives fight for power. Political parties fight for power. We all want to be lord so that we can be served by others and have things our way.

You must see this tendency in yourself and in the world around you in order to understand what it means to be a servant of others because Jesus aims His words at this very matter. A mother must see that she doesn't naturally want to raise her children in the admonition of the Lord; she wants her children to serve her. That's why their disrespect doesn't make her just sad for them but angry for herself. A pastor must see that he doesn't naturally want to shepherd his church; he wants his church to serve him. That's why he has trouble distinguishing God's plan from his own dreams and impulses.

These leaders are all called to walk the same path: humility, humiliation, and suffering. Yet they have a steadfast friend in the Suffering Servant, who once blazed the path up the dark hill and now climbs it with them. Nothing can separate them from Him (Rom. 8:35). So they can say along with the psalmist,

> Yea, though I walk through the valley of the
>   shadow of death,
> I will fear no evil;
> For You are with me;
> Your rod and Your staff, they comfort me. (Ps. 23:4)

When we reach the path's end, every tear, heartache, and wound will be well worth it (Rom. 8:18), for "if we endure, we shall also reign with Him" (2 Tim. 2:12). Those who serve and suffer for others today like Jesus will rule the kingdom tomorrow with Jesus. This is the only path to true greatness.

We realize we're ending this book on a sober note. Believe it or not, we did that on purpose. Friend, count the cost before you put the book down and take up again the task of leading others. God Himself will wipe away every tear (Rev. 7:17). But like Jesus, we will not arrive with dry eyes. Through the tears of today and the triumphs of tomorrow, may we forever be those who fear His name (Rev. 11:18).

Discussion Questions

1. Where have you heard the term *servant leader*? What do you think people mean when they use that term?

2. Tell us of a time when you worked with a leader who often did things beneath his or her pay grade. Or of a time when you worked for a leader with a mentality of entitlement.

3. Do you know any leaders who get treated far worse than they deserve? Do you know any who have suffered physical ailments because of the stress of leadership? Talk about those situations.

4. How can leaders handle mistreatment and suffering similarly to the way Jesus did?

5. How do you need to personally prepare for the hardships and sorrows of leadership?

Benediction
Our Prayer for You and This Book

We wrote this book praying that God would raise up a generation of leaders who fear Him, who take God's authority over them more seriously than their influence or authority over others. Like many others, we're burdened by problems in leadership that have become more pointed and visible in the time we spent writing. And we believe unfolding these biblical principles could be a help in correcting our steps, in seeing God's design for leadership better fulfilled among His people.

The church cannot stand for even one more supposed "natural-born leader." No one naturally fears God; rather, He teaches the foundation of leadership to those who will listen, by the work of His Spirit. The goal, prayer, and heart of this book are that the Lord might fill the generations to come with leaders who fear Him.

These wise and trustworthy leaders who fear their Lord invigorate others like the shining beams of the morning sun, blossoming the companies, ministries, lands, and families they shine on. The world is not worthy of them. So, this is our prayer, our benediction for you: may the Lord Himself give you a trembling spirit, and may He make you faithful so that the world may likewise not be worthy of you. Amen.